ADVANCE PRAISE FOR
United States Diplomacy with North Korea and Vietnam

"This is a timely and engaging study. Michael Haas draws on his considerable experience and wide-ranging scholarship, as well as a vast literature by others, to compare American diplomacy in dealing with postwar Vietnam and with nuclear-driven North Korea. The United States got it 'right' in moving from enmity to normal relations with Vietnam which has led to beneficial political and economic results, but has failed in the case of North Korea which has led to the most serious international crisis since 1962 Cuba."

—Gary Hess, *Distinguished Research Professor of History,*
Bowling Green State University

United States Diplomacy with North Korea and Vietnam

This book is part of the Peter Lang Politics and Economics list.
Every volume is peer reviewed and meets
the highest quality standards for content and production.

PETER LANG
New York • Bern • Berlin
Brussels • Vienna • Oxford • Warsaw

Michael Haas

United States Diplomacy with North Korea and Vietnam

Explaining Failure and Success

Foreword by
Bill Richardson, former UN Ambassador
Afterword by
Johan Galtung, Sociologist

PETER LANG
New York • Bern • Berlin
Brussels • Vienna • Oxford • Warsaw

Library of Congress Cataloging-in-Publication Data
Names: Haas, Michael, author.
Title: United States diplomacy with North Korea and Vietnam:
explaining failure and success / Michael Haas.
Description: New York: Peter Lang, 2018.
Includes bibliographical references and index.
Identifiers: LCCN 2018010477 | ISBN 978-1-4331-5628-1 (hardback: alk. paper)
ISBN 978-1-4331-5631-1 (ebook pdf) | ISBN 978-1-4331-5633-5 (epub)
ISBN 978-1-4331-5634-2 (mobi)
Subjects: LCSH: United States—Foreign relations—Korea (North). |
Korea (North)—Foreign relations—United States. | United States—Foreign
relations—Vietnam. | Vietnam—Foreign relations—United States.
Classification: LCC E183.8.K7 H33 2018 | DDC 327.7305193
LC record available at https://lccn.loc.gov/2018010477
DOI 10.3726/b13478

Bibliographic information published by **Die Deutsche Nationalbibliothek**.
Die Deutsche Nationalbibliothek lists this publication in the "Deutsche
Nationalbibliografie"; detailed bibliographic data are available
on the Internet at http://dnb.d-nb.de/.

The paper in this book meets the guidelines for permanence and durability
of the Committee on Production Guidelines for Book Longevity
of the Council of Library Resources.

© 2018 Peter Lang Publishing, Inc., New York
29 Broadway, 18th floor, New York, NY 10006
www.peterlang.com

All rights reserved.
Reprint or reproduction, even partially, in all forms such as microfilm,
xerography, microfiche, microcard, and offset strictly prohibited.

Printed in Germany

CONTENTS

List of Figures		vii
List of Tables		ix
Foreword by Bill Richardson		xi
Preface		xix
Abbreviations		xxiii
Part 1.	**The Need to Normalize Relations Between Countries**	**1**
Chapter 1.	Abnormal Relations Between Countries	3
Chapter 2.	Theories of Normalization	11
Part 2.	**Intensive Case Studies**	**19**
Chapter 3.	Vietnam	21
Chapter 4.	North Korea	59
Part 3.	**Implications**	**119**
Chapter 5.	Conclusions Based on Alternative Paradigms	121
	Epilogue: North Korea and World War III	133
	Afterword by Johan Galtung	139
	Index	143

FIGURES

Figure 2.1. Deterrence Paradigm of Normalization — 12
Figure 2.2. Selectorate Paradigm of Normalization — 13
Figure 2.3. Mass Society Paradigm of Normalization — 13
Figure 2.4. Community Building Paradigm of Normalization — 14
Figure 3.1. Map of Vietnam within Southeast Asia — 54
Figure 3.2. Skyline of Hanoi, Vietnam — 55
Figure 3.3. Map of Korea within Northeast Asia — 56
Figure 3.4. Skyline of Seoul, South Korea — 57
Figure 3.5. Skyline of Pyongyang, North Korea — 57

TABLES

Table 3.1. American Negotiations with Vietnam 50
Table 3.2. Vietnamese Negotiations with the United States 52
Table 4.1. American Negotiations with North Korea 107
Table 4.2. North Korean Negotiations with the United States 113
Table 5.1. Positive and Negative Moves During Negotiations 128
Table 5.2. Fulfillment of Basic Values Before and During Negotiations 129

FOREWORD
Bill Richardson

The present book is a careful historical account of diplomatic interactions between the United States and two countries—North Korea and Vietnam. In the case of Vietnam, diplomacy eventually brought about a complete normalization of relations. North Korea has posed a more significant challenge, however, and has never reached a point where talks have served to normalize relations and bring about a lasting peace between the two countries.

Ordinarily decision-makers and the media focus on responses to immediate "breaking events" with a selective memory of past events. What the present analysis provides is a detailed chronology of the back-and-forth over decades. As a result, patterns are identified that are crucial to understanding why diplomacy sometimes fails and often succeeds.

Observers often visualize different patterns based on their policy orientations. The author, Michael Haas, identifies four theories that are most commonly applied. He finds herein that success in diplomacy is most likely when negotiators engage in unilateral reciprocated confidence-building measures. Diplomatic failure, he reports, occurs when a situation is conceived entirely in terms of power politics.

As a UN ambassador toward the end of the administration of President Bill Clinton, I experienced a variety of situations where diplomacy has been needed to mitigate conflict between adversaries. Sometimes opposing parties can conclude agreements, but the process of negotiations can be very delicate, something recounted in *How to Sweet-Talk a Shark: Strategies and Stories from a Master Negotiator* (2013). Over the years I negotiated with Fidel Castro, Hugo Chavez, Saddam Hussein, and two generations of North Korean Kims, gaining experience in securing the release of persons held in detention abroad.

Although negotiations with Vietnam provided a model for diplomatic normalization by the United States with a former enemy, as explained in the present book, the history of American diplomacy with North Korea after the armistice of 1953 follows a different path.

From the early 1990s, I have had a special interest in North Korea, which I have visited eight times. In 1994, the situation was very bad. Although earlier in the year, Pyongyang agreed to denuclearize under the Agreed Framework, in December North Korea shot down an American helicopter, jeopardizing the deal and placing the United States on the path toward possible war. The administration of President Bill Clinton then sent me to Pyongyang to negotiate. After I learned that the aircraft had strayed far inside North Korean territory on a training mission, I was able to ease the situation. I even returned with the surviving pilot and the dead pilot on the outbound plane. The Agreed Framework then continued, and for nine years North Korea stopped developing its nuclear capability.

In 1996, I accompanied officials from the U.S. State Department on a mission to secure the release of Evan Hunziker, the first American citizen ever arrested by North Korea on espionage charges. During negotiations for his successful release, which took three days, I discovered that North Korea hoped to reduce tensions thereby.

During summer 2003, a North Korean delegation asked me to meet with them to discuss concerns over hostile moves by the administration of President George W. Bush. In 2005, at the request of the Bush administration, I flew to Pyongyang to assist in the ongoing Six-Party Talks. I met another North Korean delegation in 2006, when the Six-Party Talks seemed in jeopardy. North Korea's chief negotiator, Kim Kye Gwan, invited me to Pyongyang in an official capacity to provide assistance regarding negotiations with the United States.

In January 2013, shortly after the administration of President Barack Obama expressed concern over North Korea's launch of an orbital rocket, I led a delegation of business leaders to Pyongyang with two aims. One was to encourage North Korea to pay more attention to commercial possibilities than to increasing military capabilities. The other was to visit Kenneth Bae, an American citizen who was imprisoned for "hostile" actions (leaving a bible in a public place), and to urge the government to release him, which occurred the following year.

At the request of Ohio Governor John Kasich, I tried to negotiate the release of Otto Warmbier, a Cincinnati valedictorian college graduate who arrived as a tourist but was detained in January 2016 for bringing a propaganda poster from a forbidden part of the hotel back to his room. He was arrested four days before a nuclear test, so the possibility was that he was a hostage in case new sanctions were imposed. I first went to the UN to talk to the North Korean delegates, and in September a delegation from the Richardson Center for Global Engagement, including Michael Bergman, the Center vice president, went to Pyongyang. In exchange for Otto, we offered humanitarian aid and to pay for the remains for the release of American soldiers missing in action since the Korean War, but they were silent and did not disclose his condition. Not willing to negotiate with the Obama administration, they evidently were waiting for the outcome of the 2016 election. Due to the lack of American diplomatic representation in Pyongyang, the United States could not attend to his situation on a timely basis, such as by visiting him in prison. Three Americans and one Canadian were held as "prisoners of war." We visited them when we were in North Korea, but they were held as bargaining chips.

Upon receiving intelligence about Otto Warmbier, who had been in a coma for at least a year with an unexplained brain injury, the Trump administration took advantage of the opportunity to coerce his release from North Korea. Wambier and his belongings were finally freed in June 2017, but he died nine days after reaching home in Ohio after seventeen months of imprisonment. According to the Geneva Conventions, North Korea is responsible for his mistreatment as a prisoner of war. Pyongyang allowed him to remain without medical attention in an unresponsive state—a violation of international law as well as common decency.

For fifteen months, we sought the release of Otto Warmbier, employing three simultaneous pathways, as in the past: (1) We tried to find ways to apply pressure on Pyongyang. (2) While we discussed the case with the captors, we looked for what they might be willing to exchange for the release of the hostage. (3) We also counseled families of the hostages. The threefold strategy was usually successful before, but not for Otto, so we must craft a new strategy.

In the past, you could get prisoners out in exchange for high-level visits, offering humanitarian assistance. With Kim Jong Un's father, we could make a deal on prisoners, but I was then unable to deal with this man. The United States should impose some kind of punishment on North Korea specifically for Wambier's crime of humanity.

President Barack Obama tried to reformulate a new hostage policy for the age of terrorism. The formation of the Hostage Recovery Fusion Cell (HRFC) in 2015 was a step forward because agencies and departments now share relevant information to gain the release of prisoners held by terrorists, while also notifying families informed on ongoing steps to free their relatives. However, thus far families have been frustrated in gaining information from the HRFC. Some families have hired private external negotiators, but HRFC strict rules regarding the information have not helped outside parties to make a deal for their release.

Private and public diplomacy should be employed in tandem; they will be more successful together than when they operate separately. The advantage of private diplomacy is that negotiators can be chosen who have previously cultivated personal cordiality and mutual trust with their opposite numbers. For example, representatives from my Richardson Center met with North Korean officials on more than twenty occasions to obtain Otto Wambier's release, securing vital information. I believe that a private note, asking Pyongyang to allow him to depart on humanitarian grounds, would have worked before his condition deteriorated.

Since Otto was detained, Kim Jong Un violated many humanitarian principles regarding treatment of hostages. Even today, the government has not satisfactorily explained why Otto fell into a coma. They failed to inform not only his family but also the Swedish embassy, which is a conduit for American diplomacy in Pyongyang. North Korea should reveal what happened.

Today, there are problems at several levels:

First, North Korea's nuclear capability poses a grave threat to China, Japan, South Korea, and the United States, though the situation is not yet a crisis. If war comes, collateral damage would be huge. There has been a failure of American military intelligence to anticipate increased North Korean capabilities. The United States is therefore now responding to a new situation.

The greatest danger is for something to provoke war. Miscalculation is possible. For example, North Korea might shoot at a South Korean fishing boat or fire at an American aircraft mistakenly flying into North Korean airspace. With all sides trying to out-macho each other, a mistake might be interpreted as a point of crisis and serve as a pretext for war.

Kim Jong Un enjoys a cult of personality. He does not allow criticism, especially personal attacks. We do not know what he wants or what he plans to do next. He is unpredictable. We do not know what his intentions are. Clearly, he wants to stay in power. But I think that when he knew he had the power to hit the United States with a missile, he sought to negotiate. His father was like that.

North Korea's foreign minister, Ri Yong Ho, is a reasonable guy. I have dealt with him. But the degree of his access to Kim is unknown. His intense UN speech in September 2017, which threatened to shoot at American airplanes near North Korean airspace, appeared to be a message directly from Kim Jong Un.

There is a need for a clear, bipartisan policy toward North Korea. President Barack Obama's policy of "strategic patience" obviously failed. But mixed messages have come from the Trump administration.

American policy toward North Korea, in my opinion, should involve several elements. One is to improve intelligence. Massive intelligence failure should never occur again.

Next, we must continue military exercises with South Korea. We need to be fully prepared to use our military, and North Korea should know we are ready at any time.

Third, we should develop our antimissile capability to shoot down an approaching missile before the payload is close to a target. And technology should be shared with our Asian allies.

Meanwhile, economic sanctions should be enforced. Pyongyang, nevertheless, may continue to allocate any resources they have, from taxes or trade, into their nuclear and missile programs.

Finally, diplomacy is an absolute necessity. But currently there are several barriers. The most obvious is that talks require calm interaction.

Along with former Defense Secretary William Perry, Secretary of State George Schultz, and several experts on North Korea, I signed a letter to urge President Trump to declare that the United States has no hostile intentions toward Pyongyang. The letter asked for direct negotiations with Kim Jong Un, and they finally began this year.

However, the State Department is not at full strength. An American ambassador was finally named to South Korea after a summit was planned. Assistant Secretaries have not been nominated to deal with the region.

Now that a calmer atmosphere exists, there are still problems.

Trump's proposal to cancel the agreement with Iran sent a signal to North Korea that any nuclear agreement with Washington would be fragile. The

United States might pull out at any time. The Trump administration must therefore engage in creative diplomacy.

Thanks to the Singapore summit, tensions have been defused. We also know that Kim himself is deeply involved in the negotiations. We're on a path to diplomacy, rather than military confrontation, an easing of tensions on the Korean Peninsula, because of this historic summit, the personal connection of the two leaders. Another positive is the fact that there's a process starting – a process of continued negotiations.

Several issues were discussed, but no meat on the bones of the joint declaration. On the issue of denuclearization, the United States wants North Korea to dismantle its weapons. But North Korea may only want to reduce them. We want them to abandon nuclear weapons; they want us to pull our troops out of South Korea. Neither side is likely to go that far. If the United States makes a deal with North Korea, there has to be absolute verification, inspections by U.S. inspectors and the International Atomic Energy Agency or it's going to be a senseless agreement.

Also, on positive side the remains of soldiers was discussed and hopefully that will be something where the two countries come together. On the downside, there was not enough discussion about human rights. Another issue, not discussed, is North Korea's possession and sales of biological and chemical weapons. That has to stop and be included in a comprehensive settlement. On the whole, the meeting was a slight plus. But I think Kim Jong Un got the better outcome.

Lastly, typical North Korean negotiators never tell you what they're going to do. I know the North Koreans. I've negotiated with them. They're easily agitated. You don't want them to overreact. But, at the same time, you have to stand firm with the North Koreans. They don't negotiate like we do. They don't believe in quid pro quos. They always want you to go first in a negotiation. Then, when it's their turn, they hold off. They never say yes or no. They don't at all believe in timelines. They string you along. But they're enormously well prepared. They're relentless. Honor is very important to them. This is typical of their negotiations. Nevertheless, we need to get some kind of negotiating process as a result of the summit that might lead long-term to a substantial denuclearization. Let's figure out a diplomatic, long-range strategy with timelines.

Before Kim Jong Un has to move toward denuclearization, he's going to want a big price from the United States. That will require careful diplomacy to achieve a comprehensive deal, with a settlement carefully monitored for many years. Negotiations and implementation are going to take a long time. It's a very risky gamble, but I think it's worth taking.

Trump deserves credit for advancing in a situation that has never advanced as positively as it has now. My sense is that Kim Jong Un has a broader vision than his father, even his grandfather. He seems interested in foreign assistance and handouts, mainly humanitarian assistance. His vision is more focused on rebuilding his country economically through investment, new energy grids, and infrastructure – a more private sector vision. Both Trump and Pompeo have said they are open to investing in a future North Korea, but they have ruled out foreign aid, which failed under past administrations.

The next step is for diplomats of both countries to achieve the same level of mutual trust. I hope the president lets Secretary of State Mike Pompeo lead these negotiations. There should not be too many cooks in the kitchen, too many messengers within the administration. Similarly, Kim's summit success may not change how his underlings negotiate. We do not know who the North Korean lead negotiator will be. I think there has to be a lot of follow up, a lot of work ahead. Right away, momentum-wise, I think we have to move fast.

The present book demonstrates the value of diplomacy in considerable detail. If diplomacy can succeed with a former enemy, Vietnam, then it should work with North Korea.

PREFACE

Careful American diplomacy by career officials is often sabotaged by political leaders, who have little previous experience as diplomats. One result today is a nuclear power, the Democratic People's Republic of Korea, as will be explained in the pages to follow. Yet another oddity was the decision immediately after World War II to refuse to normalize relations with the Democratic Republic of Vietnam, which had been on the same side as Washington during the war. Even more extraordinary was the American acceptance of the Khmer Rouge as the legitimate government of Cambodia during the 1980s.

During my scholarly career I was involved in interviewing, lecturing, and even lobbying regarding all three countries. The list of citations herein, which spans decades, reveals the depth of my interest in the subject. Those who wonder why I was nominated for a Nobel Peace Prize will learn some of the reasons herein.

In the case of Korea, I was first flown to Seoul in 1977 to express my view that social interaction between North and South might bring benefits to both countries, a policy that was initially regarded with skepticism and was incorporated as a chapter in my edited book *Korean Reunification: Alternative Pathways* (1989). Regarding Cambodia and Vietnam, my field research from 1988 to 1990, partly sponsored by the U.S. Institute of Peace, revealed a situation so absurd that I confronted an official appointed by President George H.W. Bush in front of several journalists to tell him that the speech that he had just given in 1989 was contradicted by interviews with diplomats of friendly countries. When that official returned to Washington, his superior heard Senator Alan Cranston of California cite me as the basis for asking pointed questions; when the hearing ended, the Bush administration was instructed to get a new policy. My essay based on those interviews appeared as a chapter in my *Genocide by Proxy: Cambodian Pawn on a Superpower Chessboard* (1991).

I then began to keep careful notes on American negotiations with North Korea and Vietnam, never expecting what might be the underlying theoretical explanations. I was stunned when I counted my compilation of moves to escalate or de-escalate, as presented herein in Table 5.1. In other words, I had no bias beforehand as to the conclusions that would emerge from the quantification.

Fortunately, the situation improved regarding Cambodia and Vietnam. Eventually a new president of South Korea adopted the policies that I advanced during my trip in 1977. But later Washington double-crossed Pyongyang so many times that nuclear weapons development became inevitable and seemingly irreversible.

Yet in 2017, when I tried to urge negotiations to ease the situation and reverse warmongering from the Potomac, nobody would listen—even mild letters to the editor were rejected by the Los Angeles Times, and op-eds similar to the Epilog in the present book were rejected by the Los Angeles Times and the New York Times. Elizabeth Saunders of the Monkey Cage section of the Washington Post was the most hostile, characterizing my efforts to provide facts to dispel misconceptions as "op-eds." while publishing nonfactual op-ed essays instead. I discovered that she was so ideologically addicted to what I call the Deterrence Paradigm that she rejected the Community Building Paradigm and threw cold water on the June 12 summit even before Kim and Trump met. Nevertheless, my essays ended up on *antiwar.com*. The most disappointing was Fareed Zakaria's *The Two Faces of Kim Jong Un*, which he concludes falsely and without evidence that North Korea "cheated often." On the contrary, he showed how Congress was the biggest cheater of all by torpedoing the Agreed Framework of 1994.

The present book is an effort to explain how and why the United States eventually normalized relations with Cambodia and Vietnam, while the situation worsened in the case of North Korea. In the latter case, this book may be seen as an equivalent to what Daniel Ellsburg did in bringing facts to light in order to end the foolish American military role in Vietnam. The evidence shows that the United States has violated many agreements, whereupon North Korea considered them void, and then Washington accused Pyongyang of violations without taking responsibility for prior deviousness. Today, thanks to the Singapore Declaration of June 12, 2018, the time has come for the United States to engage in serious diplomacy to resolve issues on which the peace of the world depends.

Accordingly, I invited William Blaine "Bill" Richardson III to write the Foreword because he has practiced serious diplomacy, as he already has in roles as UN ambassador for the United States, New Mexico governor, U.S. Interior Secretary, and successful mediator in Pyongyang on five occasions. Mr. Richardson has been nominated three times for a Nobel Peace Prize.

I also invited highly influential Norwegian sociologist Johan Galtung, founder of the International Peace Research Association and the Journal of Peace Research, to write an Afterword. Also a Nobel Peace Prize nominee, he has held views on U.S. foreign policy that may seem unique in Washington but in fact should remove the shades from American eyes about how many throughout the world perceive Washington's role in world politics. I selected Galtung because he could provide a challenging overview on United States diplomacy beyond both North Korea and Vietnam. And he does—perhaps more eloquently than any scholar today.

I also thank Shutterstock for supplying images for the middle of the book.

The reader, of course, is the final judge whether the following analysis compels a re-examination of how American foreign policy is conceived as well as conducted. Identifying success in dealing with Vietnam is in sharp contrast with past failure in regard to North Korea. Accordingly, I have provided charts with details on positive and negative moves by both sides (Tables 3.1, 3.2, 4.1, 4.2, and 5.1), with sources cited at the end of each chapter. An Epilogue is provided to comment on the dangerous tension regarding relations between North Korea and the United States. The quest for success rather than failure should unite the interest of all readers, who have the last say in judging what is presented herein.

Michael Haas

ABBREVIATIONS

ADB   Asian Development Bank
AP   Associated Press
AT&T   American Telephone and Telegraph
BBC   British Broadcasting Corporation
CA   California
CBS   Columbia Broadcasting System
CNN   Cable News Network
CO   Colorado
CPPL   chosen people on chosen land
DC   District of Columbia
DMZ   demilitarized zone
DPAA   United States, Department of Defense POW/MIA Accounting Agency
DPRK   Democratic People's Republic of Korea
DRK   Democratic Republic of Kampuchea
FAO   Food and Agricultural Organization of the United Nations
FEER   Far Eastern Economic Review
HRFC   Hostage Recovery Fusion Cell

IAEA	International Atomic Energy Agency
ICBM	intercontinental ballistic missile
IIE	International Institute of Education
KEDO	Korean Energy Development Organization
MA	Massachusetts
MAC	Military Armistice Commission
MD	Maryland
MIA	soldier missing in action
MIT	Massachusetts Institute of Technology
NATO	North Atlantic Treaty Organization
NC	North Carolina
NDS	national defense system of South Korea
NJ	New Jersey
NK	North Korea
NNSC	Neutral Nations Supervisory Commission
NPT	Nuclear Non-Proliferation Treaty
NV	North Vietnam
NY	New York
NYT	New York Times
ODP	Orderly Departure Program
PAVN	People's Army of Vietnam
PBS	Public Broadcasting System
POW	prisoner of war
PRC	People's Republic of China
ROC	Republic of China
ROK	Republic of Korea
SK	South Korea
SRV	Socialist Republic of Vietnam
UK	United Kingdom of Great Britain and Northern Ireland
UN	United Nations
UNDP	United Nations Development Program
UNHCR	United Nations High Commissioner for Refugees
UNTAC	United Nations Transitional Authority for Cambodia
UPI	United Press International
U.S.	United States of America
USA	United States of America
USAID	United States Agency for International Development

USIRP	United States–Indochina Reconciliation Project
USS	United States Steamship
USSR	Union of Soviet Socialist Republics
V	Vietnam
WHO	World Health Organization

PART 1

THE NEED TO NORMALIZE RELATIONS BETWEEN COUNTRIES

The principle of diplomatic recognition developed after the Peace of Westphalia of 1648 (Fabry 2010). In an ideal world, states will have diplomatic relations with one another without restrictions. Instances of deliberate nonrecognition are anomalies which indicate conflicts that may threaten to destabilize the international system.

Currently, several small countries that claim sovereignty are not universally recognized—Abkhazia, Adzharskaya, Artsakh, Kosovo, Republic of China (Taiwan), Sahrawi, Somaliland, South Ossetia, and Transnistria. Rivalries between major powers primarily account for the anomalies.

But larger countries play a significant role in world politics and cannot be ignored. Accordingly, the present book develops two detailed case studies to illustrate how the process of moving from nonrecognition to normalization may occur by identifying the necessary and sufficient factors involved. The analysis focuses on the most critical element—negotiations that enable former enemies to seek normal diplomatic relations, using the wisdom derived from the field of international diplomacy (Murray, Sharp, Criekmans, Wiseman, Melissen 2010).

The first chapter explains why failure to normalize relations is abnormal. The second chapter provides theoretical alternatives for explaining why relations can become normal. Part II contains a detailed account of efforts at normalization with North Korea and Vietnam, two countries where the United States has sent troops and fought wars. Part III and the Epilogue provide several surprising conclusions.

References

Fabry, Mikulas (2010). *Recognizing States: International Society and the Establishment of New States Since 1776*. New York: Oxford University Press.

Murray, Stuart, Paul Sharp, David Criekmans, Geoffrey Wiseman, and Jan Melissen (2011). "The Present and Future of Diplomacy and Diplomatic Studies," *International Studies Review*, 13 (4): 709–728.

· 1 ·
ABNORMAL RELATIONS BETWEEN COUNTRIES

World peace depends upon good relations among all countries, including professional negotiations by diplomats to resolve conflicts as they escalate. In some cases, rapprochements between countries to overcome festering conflicts can come about at the bargaining table. But failure to talk and have normal relations with other countries spells trouble. Professional diplomacy can work wonders, whereas the present analysis focuses on how abnormal relations can arise, be maintained, and either be resolved diplomatically or worsen to the point of establishing pathways to war.

Diplomatic Recognition and Nonrecognition

Normal relations between states in international relations involve reciprocal establishment of embassies and consulates, commercial and social relations, and a routine handling of communications and conflicts between governments through ordinary channels of diplomacy. Under customary diplomatic practice, states exchange diplomats with each other to facilitate normal transactions. As a precaution, diplomats are recalled from diplomatic missions when countries go to war, but they are usually sent again when peace returns. Countries that have little business with each other, even if there is no policy of nonrecognition, sometimes designate another country's embassy as a point of contact. When nonrecognition exists, but the two countries want to conduct business, an "Interest Section" or "Liaison Office" is often placed within the embassy of a friendly state in the capital of the other country. Sweden, for example, now serves as the point of contact between the Democratic People's Republic of Korea (DPRK) and the United States. Sometimes an ambassador is accredited to two states because one is much smaller than the other; for example, the American ambassador to Sri Lanka is also assigned to the Maldives.

Diplomatic recognition is sometimes withheld from a newly installed foreign government when conditions in that country are so uncertain that such an act would interfere in the internal affairs of an unstable situation or when a successor government refuses to honor the obligations of the preceding regime. Nonrecognition can be used both a sign of disapproval and as a bargaining tool to secure concessions. Diplomatic nonrecognition sometimes forces another government to change its behavior.

Cases of Nonrecognition

In the twentieth century, nonrecognition evidently was first applied by the United States as a carryover from the American invasion of the Philippines in 1898. Rather than recognizing the Philippine declaration of national independence, the United States launched military action until the Philippine resistance surrendered in 1902. Next, President William Howard Taft suspended diplomatic relations in 1909 with Nicaragua. Despite his policy of self-determination, President Woodrow Wilson refused to recognize Haïti (1915), the Dominican Republic (1916), Costa Rica (1917), México (1917), and Russia (1917). Calvin Coolidge withheld diplomatic recognition from Honduras (1924) and Nicaragua (1925).

The reason for nonrecognition in the early instances was that a new government came to power by undemocratic means. Nonrecognition was a short-term policy until the Soviet Union emerged in 1917 from the former government of imperial Russia and consolidated power. Many capitalist countries in the world withheld recognition out of opposition to the nature of the new Communist government in Moscow, which announced that it would not pay off debts of the Tsarist autocracy.

From 1949, when the People's Republic of China (PRC) asserted hegemony over the China mainland, some countries continued to maintain embassies in Beijing, while others preferred diplomatic contact with the Republic of China (ROC) in Taipei, and some recognized both countries. The United States considered the PRC to be a Cold War enemy after Beijing's army entered the Korean War on the side of North Korea, and subsequently the two countries were at odds for two decades. However, efforts to achieve normalization began in 1971, when Washington stopped vetoing the PRC's application to become a member of the United Nations. Full normalization did not occur until 1979, when the United States agreed to withdraw formal diplomatic ties from the ROC.

After the end of the Cold War, the Republic of Korea (ROK) established normal relations with China and countries of Eastern Europe. Although both Koreas became members of the United Nations in 1991, and the United States has held diplomatic conversations with representatives of the DPRK from time to time since 1953, normalization between Pyongyang and Washington has not yet occurred, much to the chagrin of the North.

Although Hồ Chí Minh was on the same side as the United States during World War II in opposing Japan, Washington gave a green light to France to re-impose colonial rule over Vietnam after the war, so diplomatic recognition of Vietnam was withheld. When Hanoi prevailed in an independence war with France, a peace treaty was signed in 1954 in which Washington agreed to a temporary border between North and South, along with a plebiscite to determine whether those living in the North and South wanted unification or to form separate governments. But such a vote was never held. The United States instead recognized the Republic of Vietnam in the South and refused to exchange diplomatic missions with the Democratic Republic of Vietnam in the North. Thereafter, civil war emerged, and the United States supported the South militarily until 1973, when a peace treaty was drawn up. However, full diplomatic recognition did not occur between the United States and unified Vietnam, renamed the Socialist Republic of Vietnam (SRV), until 1995.

After Fidel Castro led a revolutionary army to overthrow the Cuban government, then ruled by Fulgencio Batista, the new government in Havana nationalized foreign businesses in 1959 and refused to compensate the owners in the United States and elsewhere. Washington then not only cut diplomatic ties but also organized a boycott of the government. In 2015, President Barack Obama recognized that the boycott was neither being honored by other countries nor was serving any purpose other than isolating the United States on the issue, so diplomatic normalization was arranged after back-channel negotiations, though many issues remain on the agenda for resolution before full normalization between the two countries.

In 1975, when the Khmer Rouge overthrew the Cambodian government, American embassy personnel fled Phnom Penh quickly. After Pol Pot's government repeatedly attacked Vietnam, Hanoi ordered the army of Vietnam to drive out the Khmer Rouge and allow a new government, the Democratic Republic of Kampuchea (DRK), to form. Because Washington believed that the DRK remained under the thumb of Vietnam, American diplomatic recognition of the new Cambodian government was withheld until a peace conference in Paris during 1991 agreed to have the United Nations enter the country to prepare for elections in order to legitimate a new government. In 1992, the American embassy was finally reoccupied, primarily to support the UN effort.

In 1979, amid chaos in Tehran, the American embassy was taken over by anti-American Iranians, who held diplomats hostage for 444 days. Although they were finally released in 1980 through secret diplomacy arranged by newly elected President Ronald Reagan, Iranian assets were frozen by Washington, and the two countries declared each other as enemies. When Iran began to develop the capability to establish nuclear power plants and potentially an atomic bomb, economic sanctions were imposed. In 2015 negotiations began, seeking a suspension of the nuclear program in exchange for a lifting of sanctions. When an agreement was reached, however, diplomatic recognition did not resume, as many points of contention have remained.

Consequences of Nonrecognition

Costs flow from nonrecognition. When two countries do not have normal diplomatic relations, the ordinary presumption is that they are technically if not actually at war, and world peace is in jeopardy. Reviewing the cases just cited, the United States has been consistently adverse to leftist revolutions around the world. That most nonrecognition occurred in the Americas was a function of the Monroe Doctrine, in which Washington assigned itself the role of policing Latin America, especially after American businesses established in some cases a dominant economic presence. Whenever American economic interests were threatened, pressure to send troops was applied.

The detention of two Americans in Nicaragua during 1909 was the pretext for canceling diplomatic recognition by Washington, though restored the following year. Disputes between conservative and leftist factions in the politics of the country drew in American interventions from 1912 to 1925 and again from 1927 to 1933 (Langley 1983), when President Franklin Delano Roosevelt instituted the Good Neighbor policy. Nevertheless, past American opposition to the leftists has soiled attitudes of many Nicaraguans toward the United States.

Soon after being sworn in as president, Woodrow Wilson announced that the United States would not recognize any government in Latin America that came to office by undemocratic means. In 1915, when the president of Haïti was assassinated, American troops rushed in to occupy the country, justified in part as thwarting a possible German takeover, and did not leave until 1934, when the Good Neighbor Policy went into effect (Schmidt 1995). Later interventions in 1965 and 1994 and efforts to bar refugees from the country during the 1990s have muddied relations.

Next came the Dominican Republic, where troops were sent after a coup in 1916. The military occupation continued until 1924. Newly elected president Warren Harding had campaigned to end the occupation, but the orders to leave were finally issued by his successor, Calvin Coolidge (Calder 1984). Yet another occupation in 1965 soured relations.

When a coup occurred in Costa Rica during 1917, Wilson refused to recognize the government, though the American government continued to maintain a diplomatic mission in the country. Despite efforts within his administration to extend recognition to the pro-American government, Wilson never relented (Baker 1965). Recognition came when a new administration came to power, though the new government finally fell as a result of American economic sanctions. Nevertheless, good relations have resulted as many Americans have retired there.

Wilson applied nonrecognition to Russia in 1917 because of opposition to the Communist revolution. He even collaborated with some Western European countries in sending American troops to support forces opposed to the Bolsheviks in the civil war (Fogelsong 1995). But the more serious menace of Nazi aggression prompted President Franklin Roosevelt to normalize relations in 1933. Resentment resurfaced as the Cold War began.

Border incidents between México and the United States continued from 1910 to 1919, including those involving the bandit Pancho Villa. After World War I broke out, Germany sought to aid México even though the United States was then formally neutral in the European war. In 1914, Wilson sent troops to the port of Veracruz to stop the flow of German arms to the government. An intervention in 1916–1917 sought to round up Pancho Villa. The Zimmerman Telegraph, intercepted in 1917, contained a German proposal for an alliance with México, whereupon diplomatic recognition was withdrawn; the prospect of an enemy on the southern border was considered intolerable. The Coolidge administration reestablished recognition in 1923, when the two countries signed a treaty according rights to American interests in the country (Kline 1961). Thereafter, relations improved despite lingering anti-Americanism. But the high point regarding México, the invitation to join the trilateral North American Free Trade Association in 1994, came crashing down as Donald Trump insisted on building a wall between the two countries.

Although American Marines entered Honduras in 1903 and 1907, fraudulent elections followed by civil unrest led to nonrecognition of the government in 1924 (Schulz and Schulz 1994). Troops entered again in 1925 to stabilize the situation, and recognition was restored. In the American conflict with Nicaragua during the 1980s, the United States assisted Honduras and has remained on friendly terms to the present.

During the Cold War, nonrecognition of China, Cuba, North Korea, and North Vietnam was a symbol of the conflict. China's growing prosperity, some derived from purchase of U.S. Treasury bonds, means that the country is far too powerful to be bullied as in the past. The American embassy in Havana has reopened but hostility and sanctions remain. In the case of the DPRK, which drew military support from China during the Korean civil war, the war has never officially ended and might resume at any time.

The consequence of refusing to recognize Hanoi was American involvement in a civil war, at first with small forces and later with hundreds of thousands of troops, ending in a peace agreement in 1973 and eventual official unification of the country in 1976. When full diplomatic recognition was restored in 1995, the United States in due course became an ally of Vietnam, as the two countries share hostility toward China.

Although the United States recognized the independence of Cambodia up to 1975, when the American embassy closed as the Khmer Rouge seized power, the result of withholding diplomatic recognition from the new government in Phnom Penh—and refusal to allow United Nations peacekeepers—was an extended proxy war from 1975 to 1991, when a multilateral agreement cleared the way for the United Nations to establish temporary control so that elections would legitimate a new government (Haas 1991a, 1991b). That new government eventually turned out to be much the same as the one not recognized from 1975 to 1991, though with a loyal opposition able to contest elections.

Implications

The consequences of nonrecognition have not always been favorable to the United States or, for that matter, to the countries so treated. There is always a memory of hostility among those affected for at least a generation. In Latin America, the residue of past interventions has not been forgotten. However, China has quietly asserted dominance in the South China Sea. Russia, having expanded into Georgia and the Ukraine, engaged in cyberwar with the United States during the 2016 election. And Pyongyang has engaged in saber-rattling, often in response to the same from Washington. Iran may go the route of North Korea unless more diplomacy achieves normalization.

The need to maintain normal diplomatic relations seems obvious, but sometimes the path is difficult. The question is "How to normalize?" Several theories abound, as discussed in the following chapter.

References

Baker, George W., Jr. (1965). "Woodrow Wilson's Use of the Non-Recognition Policy in Costa Rica," *The Americas*, 22 (1): 3–21.

Calder, Bruce J. (1984). *The Impact of Intervention: The Dominican Republic During the U.S. Occupation of 1916–1924*. Princeton, NJ: Markus Wiener.

Fogelsong, David S. (1995). *America's Secret War Against Bolshevism: U.S. Intervention in the Russian Civil War*. Chapel Hill: University of North Carolina Press.

Haas, Michael (1991a). *Cambodia, Pol Pot, and the United States*. New York: Praeger.

Haas, Michael (1991b). *Genocide by Proxy: Cambodian Pawn in a Superpower Chessboard*. New York: Praeger.

Kline, Howard F. (1961). *The United States and Mexico*. Cambridge, MA: Harvard University Press.

Langley, Lester D. (1983). *The Banana Wars: An Inner History of American Empire, 1900–1934*. Lexington: University of Kentucky Press.

Schmidt, Hans (1995). *The United States Occupation of Haiti, 1915–1934*. New Brunswick, NJ: Rutgers University Press.

· 2 ·

THEORIES OF NORMALIZATION

Instances of diplomatic efforts to move from deliberate nonrecognition to achieve mutual diplomatic recognition are a crucial subset of the study of rapprochement (cf. Rock 1989; Kacowitz 1998; Kacowitz, Bar-Simon-Tov, Elgstrom, Jerneck 2000; Kupchan 2011; Darnton 2014). Another related focus of study is of the willingness of parties engaging in military conflict to negotiate peace agreements (Ghosn 2010). In the former case, conclusions vary depending on whether parties are allies, rivals, the intensity of the dispute, and changes in leadership. In regard to the latter concern, the principal finding is that newly installed leaders are more likely to make the concessions necessary to enter into negotiations and to make them succeed than longtime leaders who often stick to previous positions. However, the cases analyzed herein follow a different pattern.

Within the study of normalization and rapprochement, alternative paradigms compete for acceptance, challenging scholars to provide evidence to accept, advance, or refute them. Two involve variants of the Rational Choice Paradigm—the Deterrence and Selectorate paradigms. A third is the Mass Society Paradigm, and the final theory is the Community Building Paradigm. Although paradigmatic claims can be diagrammed (Figures 2.1–2.4), authors of the Rational Choice variants rarely consider historical progression in causal terms or the black boxes represented by the arrows.

Deterrence Paradigm

The first Rational Choice variant, the Deterrence Paradigm, views the shift from nonrecognition to normalization through a lens in which national economic and military power is the key element (Figure 2.1). If the two countries remain equally strong, are able to deter each other through mutual threats, and a mutual threat emerges, then a marriage of convenience may occur. They may then become "frenemies." Alternatively, if one of the pair is weaker and no longer poses a threat to the stronger, they can also become "frenemies," but the weaker will concede to the stronger. The decline may be due to a dramatic shift in the power configuration, such as loss of an ally (Goertz and Diehl 1995; Bennett 1996, 1997); war devastation or civil war (Colaresi, Rasler, Thompson 2007); or the inability to finance the continuing confrontation (Colaresi 2005). But the unilateralist Deterrence Paradigm leaves out the most essential element—diplomacy.

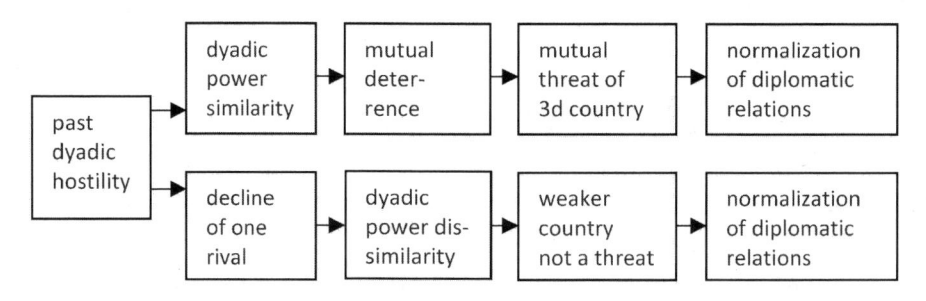

Figure 2.1. Deterrence Paradigm of Normalization.

Selectorate Paradigm

The Selectorate variant of the Rational Choice Paradigm (Figure 2.2), also unilateralist, assumes that the primary need for leaders is to stay in power as long as possible by appeasing those who have the resources to keep them in office (Bueno de Mesquita, Smith, Siverson, Morrow 2003). Normalization comes about in one of three ways:

(1) Dove leaders will be attacked for appeasement, so they will lose power if they try to normalize. When Doves are succeeded by Hawks for being too dovish, the Hawks will normalize if they can find a payoff

for their private or public selectors (Iklé 1971; Cukierman and Tommasi 1998; Colaresi 2004; Schultz 2005; cf. Cox 2010).
(2) Economic change might be central: Shifting from a planned economy to a capitalist economy may cause such disruption in furnishing private goods (for businesses) that the government will seek normalization to secure new public goods (for the general public).
(3) If a dictatorship becomes a democracy, then normalization prospects will improve (Goertz and Diehl 1995; Greig and Diehl 2006; Fehrs 2016:132) because businesses are predicted to enjoy the greater availability of private goods (Copeland 2009). However, businesses will publicize their private goods to the public as public goods (Fehrs 2016:133), usually in the form of increased jobs. Again, diplomacy is left out as if something automatic.

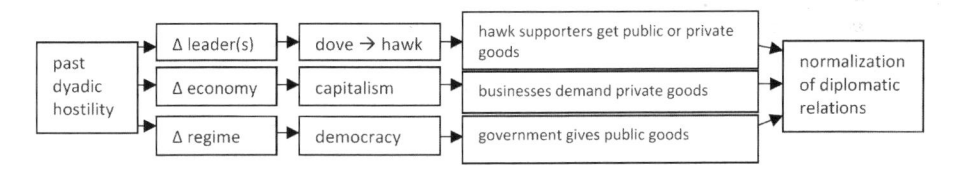

Figure 2.2. Selectorate Paradigm of Normalization.

Mass Society Paradigm

In a "mass society," the people are unable to have their needs and voices heard by those in power because intervening institutions of civil society do not work on their behalf. (Kornhauser 1959; Haas 2017a:ch7, 2017b:ch6). Normalization can occur without public input, since much foreign policy is distant from the mass public. But if the public demands or opposes normalization, government leaders are expected to follow the public mood.

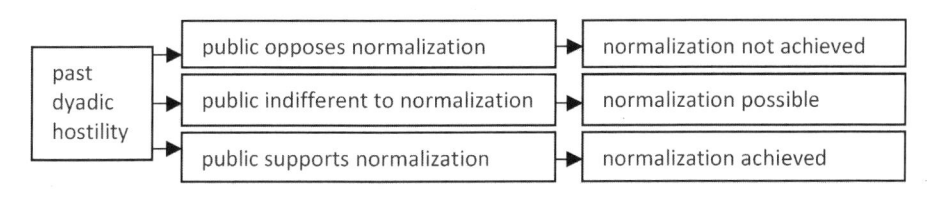

Figure 2.3. Mass Society Paradigm of Normalization.

Community Building Paradigm

The Community Building Paradigm subsumes multilateral-oriented integration and security community theories (Deutsch et al 1957; Haas 1958; Haas 2017a:ch6, 2017b:ch8). During successful diplomacy to achieve normalization, the Community Building Paradigm predicts that confidence-building measures on both sides will provide mutual assurance that neither party is a threat to the other (cf. Greig 2001) and that public goods (economic incentives) will be a guaranteed outcome during the negotiations (Darnton 2014). In short, the Community Building Paradigm goes beyond the preceding three by opening the "black box." The other paradigms blackbox diplomacy as if exogenous factors were necessary and sufficient conditions for normalization when in fact they may be necessary conditions to start diplomacy, yet diplomatic negotiations themselves constitute the sufficient condition for normalization. A key element is that the negotiators must know how to conduct diplomacy by making unilateral reciprocated concessions during or outside of talks (Rathbun 2014; Cooper 2015; cf. Holmes 2015). Alternatively stated, there is a need to develop a "common language" through diplomatic interaction in order to progress toward a positive outcome (Howard 2004).

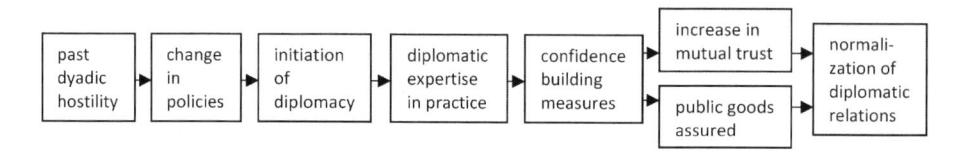

past dyadic hostility → change in policies → initiation of diplomacy → diplomatic expertise in practice → confidence building measures → increase in mutual trust / public goods assured → normalization of diplomatic relations

Figure 2.4. Community Building Paradigm of Normalization.

Other Factors in Diplomatic Negotiations

Diplomacy, of course, occurs in stages. First, two hostile countries must find a way to get to the bargaining table. During a phase known as "pre-negotiation" (Stein 1990), they pick negotiators, select a meeting site, and agree on protocol. Next come greetings, introductions, and agenda setting. Agenda setting involves identifying the subject to be discussed. In addition, the negotiators may have to meet one another for days or even months, so they must clarify how much authority they have to make an agreement—whether they must agree on general principles or work out details. Then, at the bargaining table, they must state their positions and identify options.

Other preconditions are often cited as predictors to successful negotiations for normalization of bilateral relations. Mediation, a Community-Building strategy, is usually less effective than direct bilateral talks because issues involved in normalization are too intense and thus hard to unscramble by third parties (Bercovitch and Jackson 1997; Bercovitch and Gartner 2006; Ghosn 2010:1068). Intense rivalries, involving high cost (part of the concerns in the Selectorate Paradigm), may suggest a need for negotiations, but the diplomatic outcome in such cases is usually negative (ibid., 1059).

Success in normalization negotiations requires that top leaders of both countries recognize why normalization is much more desirable that continued abnormal relations. While discussions proceed, a key element in community building is the signal that both sides are serious about proceeding toward normalization. Issues must be resolved with some confidence that they will be implemented, so mutual concessions or friendly gestures outside of negotiations indicate that progress is increasingly likely. The more past conflicts, the more difficult the negotiations. Thus, the normalization process involves overcoming many hurdles, including different cultural perspectives (Janosik 1987).

Conclusions

Enemies may not necessarily become friends or achieve a true rapprochement, but at least they may become "frenemies." A detailed examination of the process of negotiation and confidence-building measures, needed to support or reject the four paradigms, is provided in the two chapters that follow.

References

Bennett, D. Scott (1996). "Security, Bargaining, and the End of Enduring Rivalry," *International Studies Quarterly*, 40 (1): 137–183.

Bennett, D. Scott (1997). "Measuring Rivalry Termination, 1816–1992," *Journal of Conflict Resolution*, 41 (2): 227–254.

Bercovitch, Jacob, and Scott Gartner (2006). "Is There Method in the Madness of Mediation? Some Lessons for Mediators from Quantitative Studies of Mediation," *International Interactions*, 32 (4): 329–354.

Bercovitch, Jacob, and Richard Jackson (1997). *International Conflict: A Chronological Encyclopedia of Conflicts and Their Management 1945–1995*. Washington, DC: Washington Quarterly.

Bueno de Mesquita, Bruce, Alastair Smith, Randolph M. Siverson, and James D. Morrow (2003). *The Logic of Political Survival*. Cambridge, MA: MIT Press.

Colaresi, Michael (2004). "When Doves Cry? International Rivalry, Unreciprocated Cooperation, and Leadership Turnover," *American Journal of Political Science*, 48 (3): 555–570.
Colaresi, Michael (2005). *Scare Tactics: The Politics of Rivalry*. Syracuse, NY: Syracuse University Press.
Colaresi, Michael, Karen Rasler, and William Thompson (2007). *Strategic Rivalries in World Politics*. Cambridge, UK: Cambridge University Press.
Cooper, Andrew F., ed. (2015). *Diplomatic Afterlives*. Malden, MA: Polity Press.
Copeland, Dale (2009). "Trade Expectations and the Outbreak of Peace: Detente 1970–74 and the End of the Cold War 1985–91," *Security Studies*, 9 (1): 15–58.
Cox, Eric (2010). *Why Enduring Rivalries Do—or Don't—End*. Boulder, CO: Rienner.
Cukierman, Alex, and Mariano Tommasi (1998). "When Does It Take a Nation to Go to China?," *American Economic Review*, 88 (1): 180–197.
Darnton, Christopher (2014). *Rivalry and Alliance Politics in Cold War Latin America*. Baltimore, MD: Johns Hopkins University Press.
Deutsch, Karl W., Sidney A. Burrell, Robert A. Kann, Maurice Lee, Jr., Martin Lichtermann, Raymond E. Lindgren, Francis L. Loewenheim, and Richard W. Van Wagenen (1957). *Political Community and the North Atlantic Area: International Organization in the Light of Historical Experience*. Princeton, NJ: Princeton University Press.
Fehrs, Matthew (2016). "Letting Bygones Be Bygones: Rapprochement in US Foreign Policy," *Foreign Policy Analysis*, 12 (2): 128–148.
Ghosn, Faten (2010). "Getting to the Table and Getting to Yes: An Analysis of International Negotiations," *International Studies Quarterly*, 54 (4): 1055–1072.
Goertz, Gary, and Paul F. Diehl (1995). "The Initiation and Termination of Enduring Rivalries: The Impact of Political Shocks," *American Journal of Political Science*, 39 (1): 30–52.
Greig, J. Michael (2001). "Moments of Opportunity: Recognizing Conditions of Ripeness for International Mediation Between Enduring Rivals," *Journal of Conflict Resolution*, 45 (4): 691–718.
Greig, J. Michael, and Paul F. Diehl (2006). "Softening Up: Making Conflicts More Amenable to Diplomacy," *International Interactions*, 32 (4): 355–384.
Haas, Ernst B. (1958). *The Uniting of Europe*. Stanford, CA: Stanford University Press.
Haas, Michael (2017a). *International Relations Theory: Competing Empirical Paradigms*. Lanham, MD: Lexington.
Haas, Michael (2017b). *Political Science Revitalized: Filling the Jigsaw Puzzle with Metatheory*. Lanham, MD: Lexington.
Holmes, Marcus (2015). "Diplomacy after Policymaking: Theorizing Hyper-Empowered Individuals," *International Studies Review*, 17 (4): 708–710.
Iklé, Fred Charles (1971). *Every War Must End*. New York: Columbia University Press.
Janosik, Robert J. (1987). "Rethinking the Culture–Negotiation Link," *Negotiation Journal*, 3 (4): 385–395.
Kacowitz, Arie M. (1998). *Zones of Peace in the Third World: South America and West Africa in Comparative Perspective*. Albany: State University of New York Press.

Kacowitz, Arie M., Yaacov Bar-Simon-Tov, Ole Elgstrom, and Magnus Jerneck, eds. (2000). *Stable Peace Among Nations*. Lanham, MD: Rowman and Littlefield.

Kornhauser, William (1959). *The Politics of Mass Society*. New York: Free Press.

Kupchan, Charles (2011). *How Enemies Become Friends: The Sources of Stable Peace*. Princeton, NJ: Princeton University Press.

Rathbun, Brian C. (2014). *Diplomacy's Value: Creating Security in 1920s Europe and the Contemporary Middle East*. Ithaca, NY: Cornell University Press.

Rock, Stephen R. (1989). *Peace Breaks Out: Great Power Rapprochement in Historical Perspective*. Princeton, NJ: Princeton University Press.

Schultz, Kenneth (2005). "The Politics of Risking Peace: Do Hawks or Doves Deliver the Olive Branch?," *International Organization*, 59 (1): 138.

Stein, Janice Gross, ed. (1990). *Getting to the Table: The Processes of International Prenegotiation*. Baltimore, MD: Johns Hopkins University Press.

PART 2

INTENSIVE CASE STUDIES

Much has been written about normalization of diplomatic relations by the United States toward China (Kirby, Ross, Li 2006; cf. Fehrs 2016) and the Soviet Union (Richman 1980). The recent recognition of Cuba is a story of back-channel efforts that remains to be told (Zawatsky and Gemma 2015). The actual negotiation process in all three cases was much shorter than for North Korea and Vietnam, which spanned several presidential administrations and will be recounted in detail in the following two chapters.

Evidence herein is based in part on extensive interviews, as previously reported (Haas 1989, 1991a, 1991b, 2014). In addition, the diplomatic process can be pieced together from multiple sources, which are cited in the text.

Several themes will emerge in the narrative to follow. One is the puzzle of how negotiations began. In the case of China, the decision to allow "ping-pong diplomacy" opened the door. For North Korea and Vietnam, where American troops fought and died, the residue of the war had to be cleared up—for example, by locating and expatriating the dead bodies of soldiers left on battlefields.

The second puzzle is why negotiations break down from time to time. The fact is that the United States hindered progress because new presidents came to power, attached new conditions, and therefore were viewed as having double-crossed previous assurances. In the case of Vietnam, such setbacks were overcome. But Pyongyang often reacted quite sharply to Washington's apparent perfidy, and momentum was eventually lost in mutual distrust.

A third puzzle is how negotiations resume despite occasional breakdowns. One answer is that confidence-building measures are applied. Another answer focuses on the role of civil society in encouraging or discouraging continuation of negotiations. The key to any successful negotiations is the ability to see the perspective of the other side. Yet the American media have refused to present Pyongyang's vision, thereby confusing the issues for the American public.

As a result of bilateral negotiations over many years, the United States and Vietnam are quite friendly today. However, an outbreak of war between North Korea and the United States is still an option. In the latter case, each side blames the other for the current state of affairs. The reader is encouraged to compare the two sets of often tedious negotiations to ascertain why they went in different directions. Some readers may conclude that the failure of American diplomacy is primarily responsible for the fact that North Korea, which at one point had verifiably given up the development of nuclear capabilities, is now a nuclear power.

References

Fehrs, Matthew (2016). "Letting Bygones Be Bygones: Rapprochement in US Foreign Policy," *Foreign Policy Analysis*, 12 (2): 128–148.

Haas, Michael, ed. (1989). *Korean Reunification: Alternative Pathways*. 1st edn. New York: Praeger.

Haas, Michael (1991a). *Cambodia, Pol Pot, and the United States*. New York: Praeger.

Haas, Michael (1991b). *Genocide by Proxy: Cambodian Pawn in a Superpower Chessboard*. New York: Praeger.

Haas, Michael, ed. (2014). *Korean Reunification: Alternative Pathways*. 2nd edn. Los Angeles, CA: Publishing House for Scholars.

Kirby, William C., Robert S. Ross, and Gong Li, eds. (2006). *Normalization of U.S.–China Relations: An International History*. Cambridge, MA: Harvard University Press.

Richman, John (1980), *The United States and the Soviet Union: The Decision to Recognize*. Raleigh, NC: Camberleigh and Hall.

Zawatsky, Ethan, and Ashley Gemma (2015). "Diplomatic Normalization Between the US and Cuba in Light of Recent Changes in US Foreign Policy More Generally." http://digitalcommons.uri.edu/srhonorsprog/427. Accessed July 30, 2017.

· 3 ·

VIETNAM

The Imperial Army of Japan ousted French colonial forces from Vietnam during World War II. However, a resistance force led by Hồ Chí Minh fought the Japanese and in 1945 issued a declaration of independence modeled on the American counterpart of 1776. While Hồ Chí Minh read the famous words in an historic square of Hanoi, an American warplane swooped down, titled its wings in approval, and the Vietnamese cheered. The United States, in effect, was allied with the forces of Hồ Chí Minh during the final years of the war, though no diplomatic relations were ever instituted.

France, hoping to regain major power status, wanted to resume its colonial empire, including countries in Indochina. The United States, rather than continuing friendly relations with Hồ Chí Minh, gave approval to Paris to recolonize. But in 1954, Hồ Chí Minh forces soundly defeated French troops, and the French decided to leave Indochina, calling for a conference at Geneva that would spell out the terms of the new arrangement.

Three agreements, known as the Geneva Accords, were signed after months of negotiations by Britain, Cambodia, China, France, Laos, the Soviet Union, and North Vietnam (the Democratic Republic of Vietnam). The one relating to Vietnam had the following provisions: A temporary border at the 17th parallel, approximately the Perfume River, was to separate north from south, with a demilitarized zone of three miles on both sides. The government of Hồ Chí Minh was recognized as in control of the North (the Democratic Republic of Vietnam), while the former Vietnamese emperor was accepted as head of the State of Vietnam in the south, pending a plebiscite on whether Vietnamese wanted two countries or one. Hồ Chí Minh's forces (the Viet Minh) were to move to the northern side of the division, while French troops would withdraw south of the border, and neither zone would seek military allies or reinforcements. An International Control Commission of Canada, India, and Poland would monitor the agreement. Neither South Vietnam nor the United States signed the Accords; President Dwight Eisenhower later noted that some provisions could not be supported (Logevall 2012:612).

South Vietnam, supported by the United States, refused to hold elections in the south during 1956. All French forces withdrew by 1956, leaving a vacuum filled by American military advisers. Viet Minh troops covertly remained in the South, however, along with a new group, the Viet Cong. In short, the spirit of the agreement was not carried out, though the text was so ambiguously worded that "violations" may be considered misnomers (Fadiman 1997:126).

As a result, guerrilla warfare began in the South. American Special Forces were increased to support South Vietnam after 1954. Within a decade, the guerrilla movement of the Viet Cong mushroomed into a full-scale civil war. In 1965, President Lyndon Johnson authorized a massive increase in American forces to the country, and a trade embargo was imposed on North Vietnam. Negotiations to achieve a settlement of the American role in Vietnam's civil war occurred for the first time in 1968 but were unsuccessful. Hanoi sent aid to allies in the South through neutral Cambodia and Laos, prompting the United States to expand the war to all three Indochinese countries. Meanwhile, domestic support for American troops to defend a government in South Vietnam began to evaporate. Richard Nixon was elected president in 1968, promising to end the war.

After various efforts at negotiations, often just for theater (Kaiser 2016), a ceasefire agreement was finally signed at Paris in 1973, permitting American military forces to depart from South Vietnam in a manner acceptable to all sides. The signatories of the Paris Accord were the Democratic Republic of Vietnam, the Republic of Vietnam, the Provisional Revolutionary Government (representing the Viet Cong), and the United States.

Agreement Violations

According to Article 21 of the Paris Agreement on Ending the War and Restoring Peace in Vietnam of 1973, Washington pledged to "contribute to healing the wounds of war and to postwar reconstruction of the Democratic Republic of Vietnam." In another article, Hanoi promised that no more of its military forces would enter the South. To "heal" the "wounds of war" presumably meant to account for and exchange soldiers held by the other side or missing in action on battlefields.

Although President Nixon reportedly signed a letter pledging aid of at least $3 billion to secure Hanoi's approval of the agreement, Congress was in no mood to spend more on Vietnam because of the Case–Church Amendment of 1973 (U.S. Senate 1977:10). Citing American inaction on aid as a sign of perfidy, the People's Army of Vietnam used the treaty violation as a pretext for proceeding south, at first stealthily.

In April 1975, when Vietnamese troops marched into Saigon to take control of the South Vietnamese capital, Washington pointed to Hanoi's aggression as a violation of the treaty. After American embassy personnel left Saigon, ending official diplomatic relations with Vietnam, the city was renamed Hồ Chí Minh City. The trade embargo slapped on North Vietnam in 1965 remained and was then extended to the South.

Meanwhile, the Khmer Rouge took control of Cambodia in 1975 and began to assert irredentist claims to the territory of South Vietnam, which they called Khmer Krom (Southern Cambodia), even though the territory was only briefly part of the Khmer Empire several centuries earlier (Haas 1991b:ch1). In response to Khmer Rouge military attacks inside the Vietnamese border, Hanoi unified the two parts of the country in 1976, calling the new regime the Socialist Republic of Vietnam (SRV). The unification of Vietnam nonplussed U.S. officials.

Negotiations to normalize relations between the United States and Vietnam later ensued through several stages. Terms of normalization, first set by Hanoi and later by Washington, proved difficult to meet and are among the most protracted on record. An account of how the two countries managed to normalize relations over a period of two decades may serve as a useful model in examining prospects for diplomatic normalization elsewhere in the world.

Accordingly, the present chapter traces efforts to achieve normalization, focusing on specific issues in contention—living up to the peace agreement ("healing the wounds of war" and economic aid), policies toward Cambodia, as well as such humanitarian issues as the resettlement of refugees and Amerasians. In addition, the analysis demonstrates how progress toward some aspects of normalization was achieved through private sector initiatives in the fields of trade and investment, travel, and humanitarian aid. The narrative describes the "road map" presented by Washington to Hanoi in 1991 and later developments. In other words, both sides had to go beyond blaming each other for violations of the Paris Accord and engage in constructive action as well as dialog in order to achieve normalization of their commercial and diplomatic relations.

"Healing the Wounds of War"

When Vietnam's civil war ended in 1975, the body count revealed that about 1.2 million Vietnamese died, and about an equal number were disabled or wounded, of whom about 60 percent were children under the age of 16 (Small and Singer 1982:93; Oxfam America 1988:3). In contrast, the number of American deaths was only 56,000, though many more were disabled and wounded (ibidem).

Troops were also sent by American allies Australia, Canada, New Zealand, the Philippines, South Korea, and Thailand. The experience of soldiers in combat roles in Vietnam from 1965 to 1973 was fresh in the minds of those on both sides of the conflict for at least two decades, so both sides first sought the whereabouts of those who disappeared during the fog of war.

At war's end in 1975, Vietnam began the task of identifying some 300,000 of its own personnel missing in action (MIAs) through its Office for Seeking Missing Persons (Indochina Chronology 1993a:5). In the process of locating bodies, the remains of American soldiers were uncovered as well. But Washington's welching on the promise of reconstruction assistance caused Hanoi to fail to report on the first American MIAs found on battlefields.

Meanwhile, Hollywood films fed illusions by producing films about American prisoners of war (POWs) supposedly still in captivity in Vietnam. Despite repeated U.S. government denials that POWs remained, million-dollar campaigns of various "Rambo" groups, such as the American Defense Institute, sent balloons from Thailand into Indochina, offering to pay for information concerning live Americans allegedly seen, thereby tempting opportunists to fabricate photographs and stories.

When Hanoi pleaded to begin negotiations for normalization of relations in 1976, President Gerald Ford unexpectedly declared an unwelcome precondition—full accounting of Americans missing in action, including the return of any remains. Evidently, he was aware that some MIA organizations were opposing financial aid to Vietnam until their concerns were met. Hanoi did not agree, as Vietnam was still owed reparations according to the Paris agreement, and economic reconstruction was an urgent need for the devastated country. In other words, the two countries were imposing mutually unacceptable preconditions rather than moving ahead on both fronts.

After President Jimmy Carter was sworn into office in 1977, he took several conciliatory moves: Foreign airplanes and ships bound for Vietnam were allowed to refuel in the United States, travel restrictions lapsed, the U.S. Postal Service began to accept mail for Vietnam, and the United States declined to veto SRV's application for UN membership. Yet another unilateral confidence-building measure was the establishment of the Presidential Commission on Americans Missing and Unaccounted for in Southeast Asia, which dispatched a mission to Hanoi. Chair Leonard Woodcock and members of the commission were warmly received, and Vietnam soon turned over 12 bodies. The fate of at least 600 MIAs in Vietnam was then given high priority (U.S. Senate 1977:14). Hanoi next stopped linking progress on MIA issues with the requirement that aid was owing to Vietnam before full normalization talks could begin.

When Vietnam proposed a resumption of negotiations in Paris, Carter agreed. But Hanoi's diplomats insisted during three negotiation sessions that the price of normalization was some of the aid promised at the time of the Paris agreement. Since Congress was unwilling to supply aid to the former enemy, discussions foundered. Woodcock, originally assigned to normalize relations with Vietnam, then went instead to handle normalization talks with the People's Republic of China, which were concluded in 1979.

In mid-1978, Foreign Minister Nguyễn Cơ Thạch dropped American economic assistance as a precondition for normalization and obtained Washington's approval to begin talks at an unspecified date. But he soon went to Moscow to sign a friendship treaty that would bring aid, as Hanoi was planning to drive the Khmer Rouge out of Cambodia later that year and would have to finance the costs of an occupation of that country. By 1979 normalization talks were out of the question due to Vietnam's role in Cambodia, as explained below.

Progress in negotiations remained stalled after Ronald Reagan took office in 1981. Four years later, Vietnam unilaterally returned the remains of 30 American war dead, allowed the U.S. government for the first time to participate in an excavation of a suspected B-52 crash site near Hanoi, and promised to settle the MIA issue by 1987. Although the Reagan administration then proposed that resolution of the issue should be left entirely to private aid agencies, Vietnam insisted on an official representative of the American government before allowing more intensive investigation units to operate. SRV official reasoning was that Washington was responsible for sending soldiers to Vietnam, so they should be removed by the U.S. government, whereas the actual rationale was that Hanoi wanted to deal with Washington as an equal partner at the bargaining table in order to discuss normalization. By the end of 1986, however, only about 100 American remains had been identified. With little progress toward normalization, Vietnam reverted to the position that further MIA searches depended on receipt of economic aid.

A breakthrough came in August 1987, when General John A. Vessey, Jr., was sent as Reagan's personal emissary to Hanoi. Rather than taunting Vietnam on other matters, as occurred during similar meetings in the past involving State Department negotiators, Vessey made clear his desire to stick to the complex technical issue of identifying remains of war casualties. Having built confidence that negotiations would not be distracted, Vessey and Foreign Minister Nguyễn Cơ Thạch agreed that the MIA issue should be settled without preconditions or linkage with other issues involving the two countries. Thereafter, U.S. Joint Casualty Resolution Center personnel were allowed to go to Vietnam in order to track information about incidents of loss, and the U.S. Army Central Identification Laboratory sent teams of forensic experts. Within the next two years, some 263 additional remains were identified (Honolulu Advertiser 1989a, 1989b).

During August 1988, to the astonishment of many observers, Vietnam suddenly announced a "temporary suspension" in progress on the MIA issue because of an apparent change of policy in Washington—an effort to link the MIA issue with other matters, contrary to the Thạch–Vessey agreement. One example was Reagan's speech in July to the National League of Families of American Prisoners and Missing in Action in Southeast Asia, during which he misstated current policy by claiming that progress on the MIA issue awaited a new condition—withdrawal of Vietnam's army from Cambodia. On behalf of MIA groups, however, Republican Senator and Vietnam veteran John McCain had recently proposed an Interest Section for U.S. affairs at a friendly embassy in Hanoi in order to deal with MIA and related issues. But in August, Assistant Secretary of State Gaston Sigur testified against McCain's proposal in Congress. According to a Voice of America mistranslation, Sigur said that Washington would continue to isolate Vietnam until Vietnamese troops left Cambodia. For Hanoi, eager to normalize relations and to cooperate with Washington on the MIA issue on humanitarian grounds, such statements at the highest levels were so offensive as to require a negative response, so the Foreign Ministry issued the "temporary suspension" without first checking with Foreign Minister Thạch, who was out of town. The "temporary suspension," even prompted McCain to withdraw his resolution. When Thạch returned to Hanoi in early September after a one-month absence, the suspension was rescinded, and by the end of the month an American mission was allowed for the first time to search anywhere in the country and to interview rural villagers on their memories of MIAs (Brown 1989). Although the State Department turned down Thạch's generous offer in 1988 to establish as many as fifteen offices in Vietnam in order to coordinate MIA searches (Erlanger 1989), the U.S. government relented during the first year of the presidency of George H.W. Bush, and a "temporary office" at Hanoi opened during June 1991.

From 1991 to 1992, more sensational publicity suggested that Hanoi had held back some POWs after 1973 (Rosen 1992). In October 1991, for example, unidentified Soviet intelligence agents pretended on Australian television that American POWs may have been flown from Vietnam to the Soviet Union. In January 1992, Major General Oleg Kalugin, who headed Soviet counterintelligence during the 1970s, denied the latter claim but stated that in 1978 his agents questioned three Americans near Hanoi about U.S. covert operations. A Russian newspaper reported a sighting of an American sometime after 1973 in Soviet Kazakhstan. All the stories were eventually discredited, but Vietnam had to deny each one, and the U.S. government likewise repeated statements that there was no confirmed evidence of any American prisoners killed or living in captivity in Indochina. During that interregnum, Vietnam ceased cooperation on MIAs (Childress and Solarz 1998:100).

When the POW furor died down, MIAs searches continued routinely, and very few now remain unaccounted for. The wounds of war were considered healed by the time President George H.W. Bush left office in early 1993.

The Cambodian Tangle

For many years, a Cambodian cloud hung over relations between Hanoi and Washington, slowing progress (Haas 1991a, 1991b). In April 1975, the Khmer Rouge forces of Pol Pot toppled the U.S.-backed Cambodia government of Lon Nol even before American embassy personnel escaped from Saigon. Pol Pot's regime quickly aligned itself with China, drove ethnic Vietnamese out of the country, butchered or starved at least one million Cambodians, and attacked villages inside Vietnam, one coming within ten miles of Hồ Chí Minh City. In response, Hanoi complained of Cambodian aggression at the United Nations and sought assistance from the People's Republic of China (PRC) to stop the genocidal carnage. Within a year after taking power, the Khmer Rouge had already caused 30,000 deaths inside Vietnam (Lindgren, Wilson, Wallensteen 1989:6).

During March 1977, while Woodcock was in Hanoi, SRV officials asked Washington to moderate China's ongoing support for the Khmer Rouge. In August 1978, Senator George McGovern called for an international force to drive Pol Pot's genocidal regime from Cambodia. But President Carter failed to do so based on advice from National Security Adviser Zbigniew Brzezinski.

At Brzezinski's initiative, Woodcock had been negotiating with Beijing to normalize U.S.–PRC relations. Due to evidence that Vietnamese leaders visited Moscow to secure help from the Chinese-backed Khmer Rouge, Brzezinski and others believed that Hanoi had abandoned a policy of equidistance between feuding Beijing and Moscow. Hanoi, indeed, was prepared to allow increased Soviet influence in Vietnam in order to deter a possible attack from China, Pol Pot's ally. Secretary of State Cyrus Vance, aware that something should be done to stop the genocidal Pol Pot from inflicting a holocaust in Cambodia, wanted to normalize relations with Hanoi. But Brzezinski wanted to play the "China card" against the Soviet Union, and he thus considered relations with Cambodia and Vietnam to be of secondary importance. President Carter then had to choose between two advisers, and Brzezinski won out (Chanda 1986).

With no alternative but to defend the country from attack, troops of the People's Army of Vietnam (PAVN) entered Cambodia on December 25, 1978, and were immediately greeted by the Cambodian people as liberators. Citing humanitarian considerations grounded in international law in support of the intervention within Cambodia (Klintworth 1989:ch3–4), Vietnam's intervention enabled a small group of refugees from the Khmer Rouge to set up the People's Republic of Kampuchea in Phnom Penh during January 1979. The Khmer Rouge, meanwhile, took refuge along the border with Thailand. Hanoi's plea to have PAVN replaced by UN peacekeepers was blocked from the agenda of the UN Security Council (New York Times 1979).

After Brzezinski signaled approval, China attacked Vietnam in February 1979, but the Soviet Union soon forced Beijing to back down by mobilizing troops on China's northern border. As a result of Brzezinski's policy, therefore, both Beijing and Moscow expanded their military presence into Southeast Asia. By 1981, Thailand was pressured by Washington to serve as a conduit for American and Chinese aid to forces opposing PAVN so that economically weak Hanoi might tire of the war (Becker 1986:440; Humeniuk 1988). Washington then arranged for worldwide condemnation of Vietnam for invading Cambodia and for not withdrawing, even though the result might be to allow the Khmer Rouge to climb back to power. The United States also pooh-poohed SRV's claim to exercise the inherent right of self-defense, engage in humanitarian intervention, and promise to withdraw from Cambodia in favor of a UN force if promised that the Khmer Rouge would never be allowed to return to power (Haas 1991b:ch4). From 1979, therefore, the administrations of Jimmy Carter and Ronald Reagan maintained that there was a new precondition for normalization for relations with Vietnam—unilateral withdrawal from Cambodia without conditions.

When Hanoi announced in 1985 that PAVN would leave unconditionally by 1990, Washington insisted that the pullout had to be verified. During 1988, Vietnam withdrew all civilian and military advisers, having trained the army of the government in Phnom Penh. In April 1989, when Hanoi indicated that PAVN would depart by the end of September, the French government organized a peace conference at Paris during midsummer. Despite the awareness of U.S. State Department delegates to the conference that Vietnam made concessions on every issue under its control, Washington insisted that a Cambodian transitional government must include the Khmer Rouge, a condition unacceptable to most delegates. The United States then blamed the failure of the Paris conference on Hanoi. Delegates from other countries, including Australia, blamed American Vietphobia (or perhaps Khmer Rougephilia) for the failure of the conference (ibid., ch19).

When Vietnamese troops left Cambodia a few days before the end of September 1989, as promised, Hanoi believed that the final condition to start normalization talks with the United States had been fulfilled. Whereas PAVN's withdrawal served to normalize relations between China and Vietnam, Washington moved the goal posts yet again, now insisting that normalization awaited Hanoi's efforts to pressure the Phnom Penh government to accept a transitional quadripartite government that would include the Khmer Rouge. Vietnam responded that superpowers might indeed feel free to dictate how sovereign states should govern themselves, but Hanoi would not do so.

At the end of 1989, when hopes for a settlement of the Cambodian conflict seemed remote, the Khmer Rouge and non-Communist allies attacked forces of the government in Phnom Penh, bringing the Khmer Rouge closer to retaking power. When the Cambodian army held back the invading forces, Australian Foreign Minister Gareth Evans undertook to revive chances for peace by proposing a temporary United Nations authority to hold elections that would enable a new, democratically-chosen government to emerge in Cambodia.

President George H.W. Bush announced in mid-1990 that high-level contacts between the United States and Vietnam would be held to discuss terms of a Cambodian settlement. Although Hanoi agreed with the Australian plan, Bush insisted that normalization talks with Hanoi would occur only on the day after Vietnam's signature appeared on a Cambodian peace treaty. When the Paris conference reconvened in October 1991, a detailed version of Australia's plan was accepted and signed, and the new State of Cambodia came into existence. In January 1992, the American embassy in Phnom Penh reopened to participate in the transition. Formal American–Cambodian diplomatic relations resumed after elections were held for the Cambodian parliament in 1993, but normalization of relations with Vietnam was still held up.

Humanitarian Issues

While the Cambodia problem complicated relations between the United States and Vietnam, humanitarian concerns asserted themselves. Many Vietnamese wanted to leave the country, perceiving no future for themselves. There were two kinds of travelers—political refugees and economic migrants. But there were two other types of persons seeking resettlement—Amerasians and political prisoners in Vietnamese internment facilities.

Refugees

Even before 1975, many Vietnamese left their country for resettlement as refugees. Approximately 600,000 entered the United States by 1990 (U.S. Commerce Department 1993:15), and twice that number came in the next two decades (Institute of International Education 2010–12). Others left for Australia, Britain, and France. Although Chinese radio broadcasts even frightened 500,000 ethnic Chinese inside Vietnam to depart for China (Crossette 1988), many Vietnamese Chinese departed for the same destinations as the rest of the Vietnamese. Relatives of Vietnamese refugees were, of course, potentially eligible for resettlement in due course.

Although clandestine out-migration is against SVR law, many prosperous citizens were quite willing to use their wealth to bribe officials in order to leave by boat, knowing that Vietnam lacked a coast guard or sufficient navy to prevent an outflow. Taking perilous journeys, they were prepared to endure squalid refugee camps in third countries before landing in destination countries. Even less prosperous Vietnamese took their chances in makeshift vessels. In September 1988, Vietnam revealed that some 4,000 cases of illegal departure had been tried in court since 1975 (Aspen Institute 1988:7; Hanoi International Service 1988).

In the late 1970s, friends of the American government fled, fearing for their lives; as political refugees, they had a reasonable chance of being granted asylum. Pursuant to an agreement at the International Conference on Indo-Chinese Refugees at Geneva in 1979, the UN High Commissioner for Refugees (UNHCR) received permission from Hanoi to inaugurate the Orderly Departure Program (ODP), not only to facilitate immigration for those living in temporary camps in Indonesia, Malaysia, and Thailand but also to enable an efficient processing of applicants inside Vietnam in order to obviate the extreme suffering associated with hazardous, illegal departures. Under ODP, U.S. State Department personnel began to interview applicants for immigration inside Vietnam in the role of UNHCR representatives.

However, only 2,219 ODP departures to the United States occurred from October 1979 to September 1981 (Funseth 1989:2). Hanoi believed that Vietnamese emigrants were being held up by deliberate U.S. processing delays, but Washington claimed that the SRV was responsible for delays in issuing exit visas, both swipes at bureaucracies. In fact, a very limited number of American personnel was assigned to interview applicants, to process those accepted as immigrants or refugees, and to handle pre-settlement orientation programs. Efforts to find sponsors for them inside the United States were also protracted. In 1984, Vietnam briefly suspended cooperation with the United States to protest the slow processing of applicants. Objecting to continued processing at a snail's pace in 1985, Vietnam announced an indefinite suspension in 1986. With the United States still working on applicants for 1982 at a rate of about 10,000 per year, ODP could have continued until the last half of the twenty-first century. Accordingly, some applicants became discouraged and left by boat (Albor 1990).

With the arrival of General Vessey in Hanoi during 1987, the situation changed. Although Vessey was originally dispatched only to handle the MIA issue, he later addressed related matters. In July 1987, a bilateral agreement was finally worked out between the two countries. But when Hanoi complained that U.S. processing was still not keeping up with the rate of applications, the U.S. State Department leased an office in Hồ Chí Minh City during November 1988.

In mid-1989, Washington announced a goal of 3,500 interviews per month, a shift in policy that was long overdue. Vietnam, for its part, promised to increase the rate of exit visas to 20,000 per year (Hiebert 1988b; Chapon 1989). Washington also agreed to accept 22,000 of the 55,000 Vietnamese from refugee camps elsewhere in Southeast Asia (Funseth 1989; Yu, Pregelj, Suiter 1989:10).

Economic Migrants

Economic migrants emerged increasingly as the U.S. trade embargo crippled the Vietnamese economy. With little chance of qualifying for entry into the United States or any other country under immigration and refugee resettlement laws, they took perilous voyages to escape poverty and became known as "boat people." Some Vietnamese also took bus rides to China, where they purchased boats for a short voyage to Hongkong.

In October 1988, the SRV for the first time participated in multilateral discussions on problems of the "boat people" during a meeting including representatives from British Hongkong, Laos, and countries of the Association of South-East Asian Nations (Brunei, Indonesia, Malaysia, the Philippines, Singapore, and Thailand). In late 1989, with some 58,000 Vietnamese in detention centers within Hongkong, Britain was forcibly repatriating the economic migrants by placing them in airplanes, having made arrangements with Hanoi for their resettlement and non-prosecution for illegal departure (Reuters 1990). In 1989, discussions during the International Conference on Indo-Chinese Refugees at Geneva bore fruit in the form of a Comprehensive Plan of Action, in which Vietnam agreed to accept the voluntary return of Vietnamese "boat people."

Amerasians

After 1975, immigration to the United States excluded some 20,000 of those born of American fathers and Vietnamese mothers out of wedlock (Funseth 1989:3). Many "Amerasians," including those with African American fathers, had a difficult time leading a normal life in Vietnam due to social prejudice more than government policy. Their plight was brought to American consciousness through accounts from the mid-1990s by visitors who stayed at the

Rex Hotel in Hồ Chí Minh City, where they begged in front for attention to ease their situation.

Initially, the U.S. State Department did not allow Amerasians to be eligible for immigration under UNHCR's ODP criteria. Hanoi insisted that fathers should return to Vietnam to claim their children, as a case of mistaken identity might occur if the latter were flown out unaccompanied. Other delays were imposed because Vietnam thought that the Amerasian issue was a "war legacy" which should be handled through bilateral negotiations with Washington rather than through UNHCR. After repeated criticisms for failing to deal on a bilateral basis with the SRV on the matter, the State Department announced a special Amerasian "sub-program" within the U.S. ODP in September 1984, and Vietnam responded by allowing a significant increase in Amerasians for emigration to the United States (Goose and Horst 1988).

As mentioned above, Hanoi temporarily suspended the outflow of Vietnamese in 1986, including Amerasians. Representatives Robert Mrazek and Thomas Ridge, both Vietnam-era veterans, then introduced the American Homecoming Bill in August 1987 in an effort to achieve a compromise. The bill was designed to accept Hanoi's preference to handle the arrangement bilaterally and to classify Amerasians and immediate family members as "immigrants" rather than "refugees," while satisfying the State Department's insistence on face-to-face interview by American immigration officials and a program for basic resettlement services to ease adjustment to life in the United States. The bill, signed by President Reagan just before Christmas 1987, placed a deadline for the departure of all Amerasians by March 21, 1990, and authorized $5 million to pay for estimated costs.

Before the Homecoming Bill passed, some 4,000 Amerasians and 5,500 close relatives had already arrived in the United States (ibid.; Belkin 1988; UPI 1988). During the first year of the operation of the Amerasian program, some 15,000 were interviewed, 5,000 departed, and 25,000 left by mid-1990 (Moore 1990). About 80 percent of the Amerasians interviewed were approved on the spot.

Political Prisoners

In 1975, many officials of the Republic of Vietnam and soldiers in its army were unable to leave when U.S. embassy personnel and friends departed. The Hanoi government rounded up about thousands of "collaborators" from the former regime for purposes of political re-education. Contrary to predictions of a bloodbath, they were not executed, though conditions in the re-education camps were severe. Lower-level personnel were released first, but at least 1,000 remained in detention as late as 1987, perhaps unconvinced that the Socialist Republic of Vietnam was the legitimate ruling authority in the country.

Many living in the United States were aware of the plight of the political prisoners, especially relatives and close friends. The SRV claimed that the issue was negotiable as early as 1982, and Heritage Foundation and the National Unified Front for Liberation of Vietnam pressed the U.S. government to do so. But Washington claimed that Hanoi was unwilling to negotiate the matter (Funseth 1989:3).

In September 1987, when the MIA dialog began to bear fruit, Foreign Minister Thạch indicated a willingness to allow political prisoners to leave for the United States on two conditions—an American pledge to refrain from supporting subversive activities conducted against the SRV and the beginning of humanitarian aid to Vietnam. In mid-1989, Secretary of State James Baker III opened negotiations on the subject. After Thạch dropped both preconditions, an agreement was announced in July. Some 3,000 former prisoners and their close relatives left for the United States by the end of the year (Chapon 1989). Another 1,000 emigrated to the United States in 1989, and almost 38,000 left by June 1992, when all remaining political prisoners were released from detention (Albor 1990; Indochina Chronology 1992:7).

Economic Issues

Hostile intergovernmental relationships between the United States and Vietnam had consequences for nongovernmental interactions. The American government, obsessed with power politics during the Cold War, discouraged travel, and prohibited humanitarian aid as well as economic transactions involving all Communist countries. Government policy remained quite consistent over time, but private American citizens tried to build bridges with Vietnam and even provided some economic input to the country while promised governmental aid was still being denied.

Travel

The trade embargo served to discourage travelers from going to Vietnam, though American restrictions on travel were lifted in 1977. In 1978, Professor

Edward Cooperman of California State University at Fullerton and others founded the U.S. Committee for Scientific Cooperation with Vietnam with the aim of renewing ties between scholars and scientists of the two countries. Entry into Vietnam then required clearance from several ministries as well as the Prime Minister on behalf of the Council of Ministers. Visas were generally secured from the SRV embassy in Bangkok, and trips to Vietnam were booked in Bangkok as well. Air tickets were purchased from Air France, Air Vietnam, and Thai International. No American flag carriers then flew to Hanoi or Hô Chí Minh City.

More regular travel from Vietnam to the United States began in 1981 during the era of President Reagan, when the Vice Rector and a University of Hanoi geographer visited the East–West Center and the adjacent University of Hawai'i. In 1982, a group of Vietnamese scholars attended a conference of the Association for Asian Studies held within the continental United States. In 1983, Cornell University invited a historian from Vietnam to teach as a Visiting Professor for two months, the maximum interval of time then allowed by the State Department for citizens from Vietnam in the United States. By the mid-1980s, visitors to Vietnam found that the government and the people did not manifest enmity toward the United States

In 1985, several American journalists successfully applied for permission to go to Vietnam on assignments that would commemorate the ten-year anniversary of the evacuations from the American embassy in Saigon. In addition, the U.S.–Indochina Reconciliation Project (USIRP) began the first of several semiannual study tours, primarily for academics, in 1985.

Before 1985, most tourists in Vietnam came from Eastern Europe or the Soviet Union. With the advent of Mikhail Gorbachëv's perestroika in 1986, Eastern Europeans were free to travel to Western Europe, so Vietnam needed to make up for the tourism shortfall and to obtain foreign exchange by encouraging Westerners to travel as tourists. By 1988, there were plenty of air-conditioned busses, curio shops, English-speaking guides, maps, and Ministry of Tourism brochures catering to American and Western European tourists.

Although many Vietnamese expatriates wanted to return to visit relatives, only 2,000 tourists arrived from the United States in 1988. Many Vietnamese Americans feared that right-wing Vietnamese would harass them with death threats upon their return (Brazaitis 1989; McAuliff 1989). In fact, Cooperman had been shot in 1984 by a Vietnamese immigrant. Those who made the trip often brought clothing, medicines, video recordings, and other goods, many of which were subsequently traded by their relatives on the open market.

The year 1988 also heralded the first time a student from the United States was allowed to study in Vietnam, when a University of Hawaiʻi student enrolled at the University of Hanoi. During the same year, Georgetown University and the University of Hawaiʻi led the first student tours to Vietnam.

But in June 1989, after the election of President George H.W. Bush, American permission for a University of Utah study tour was denied, and Lindblad Travel of Westport, Connecticut, was fined $80,000 for arranging a tour of Cambodia and Vietnam without first applying for a Treasury Department license (Cerquone 1989). When USIRP applied for a license to avoid a similar fate, the U.S. government imposed new restrictions, including the requirement to report names of all travelers, but granted the license anyway. The war with Vietnam, thus, lived on, with the American government harassing its citizens once again.

But in 1991, Washington lifted all travel restrictions and authorized the U.S. Information Agency to begin exchange programs with Vietnam. Nowadays, students from Vietnam form the eighth largest group of international students in the United States (IIE 2012–12).

Humanitarian Aid

The need for humanitarian aid to Vietnam was clear (cf. Minear 1988; Oxfam America 1988:2). The war left some 300,000 Vietnamese disabled, of whom about 60,000 needed artificial limbs, and at least 500,000 were orphans. More than 16 million gallons of Agent Orange and other chemicals were dumped on Vietnam during the 1960s, resulting in 500,000–1,000,000 birth defects by the end of the century (York and Mick 2008; King 2012), the destruction of more than one-third of the mangroves, and the defoliation of some 5.4 million acres (the size of Massachusetts) of farmland and forest (Borg 1988). About 25 million bomb craters compressed the soil to rocklike hardness. Women in the south were estimated to have the world's highest levels of dioxin in breast milk, and the incidence of birth defects was probably the highest in the world (Oxfam America 1988:3). By the mid-1990s, some 56,000 Vietnamese died while running into land mines and unexploded bombs; others were disabled.

The American embargo of aid and trade affected many private voluntary organizations, including the American Friends Service Committee, which provided aid in South Vietnam before 1975. Such groups as the Mennonite Central Committee stayed in the country to conduct needs assessment but could not provide aid because Washington interpreted the Trading with the Enemy Act to proscribe all financial dealings with Vietnam.

After the United States allow SRV to be admitted to the United Nations in 1977, four UN aid agencies (FAO, UNDP, UNICEF, WHO) began to operate in Vietnam, providing about $75 million in annual assistance during the 1980s (Minear 1988). The Soviet Union, in contrast, provided some $2 billion annually during the same decade (UK 1988:5). Sweden, then second major donor after the Soviet Union, reassessed its aid in 1975 and decided to sponsor a medical assistance project throughout the country. The United States could not interfere with such bilateral or multilateral aid.

Instead, the U.S. government severely restricted items that could be shipped to Vietnam from American sources. In 1981, Washington initially denied a license for schoolchildren to ship paper and pens to Vietnamese schools. But the license was granted after they wrote President Reagan for permission to do so at Christmastime (Minear 1988:6).

Following his trip to Hanoi in 1987, General Vessey recommended that private aid be allowed so as to encourage Vietnam to implement the MIA agreement, a recommendation accepted by Reagan as an effort to "help accelerate a process of healing" (ibid., p. 1). An American aid organization then donated sewing machines, purchased in Singapore, for a school in Hồ Chí Minh City; in another act of charity, some $500,000 in wheelchairs was donated (ibid., p. 5).

Oxfam America was one of ten private charitable organizations finally granted a license by the Treasury Department to operate in Vietnam, initially during 1988, when approximately $4.5 million in unofficial aid went from the United States to Vietnam (ibidem). In late 1989, the Bush administration decided to send $250,000 worth of surplus government medical equipment through nongovernmental channels as a reward for Hanoi's cooperation in locating MIAs (Honolulu Advertiser 1989c).

Among the earliest humanitarian projects originally proposed by the State Department, a group of veterans constructed medical facilities during 1990 in a Vietnamese village where they earlier had inflicted casualties. Contact between veterans on both sides promoted psychological healing, according to the veterans; one of the clinics was designed to service more than 100,000 Vietnamese (Hatfield 1990). Then in 1991, the U.S. Agency for International Development (USAID) resumed humanitarian aid. By mid-1994, USAID provided $7.4 million in assistance to children, orphans, and civilian war victims though contracts with private voluntary organizations (Morse 1994).

Trade and Investment

Under the terms of the Trading with the Enemy Act of 1917, trade with North Korea was banned during the 1950s. In 1964, for the same reason, the United States banned all commercial transactions with North Vietnam. In April 1975, when South Vietnam fell, the trade embargo imposed on the North was extended to the South, and all Vietnamese assets were frozen in American banks. Yet the United States promised economic aid to Vietnam under the Paris agreement of 1973.

Two months after Hanoi's victory in 1975, Premier Phạm Văn Đồng invited the United States to normalize relations with Vietnam, provided that Washington would honor the commitment in the Paris Accord to provide funds for reconstruction. Bank of America and First National City Bank were invited to discuss the possibilities of trade, and American oil companies were encouraged to apply for concessions to search for oil in Vietnamese waters. But Congress, under the Case–Church Amendment of 1973, refused to allow any assistance. Vietnam's alliance with the Soviet Union in 1978 meant that neither aid would flow nor normalization talks would begin.

Over Washington's objections, the World Bank lent some $60 million to Vietnam in 1978 to support economic reforms. But after PAVN entered Cambodia at the end of the year, there was no chance of any more disbursements on the loans. Hanoi, in turn, stopped paying interest on an earlier stand-by loan from the International Monetary Fund (IMF) of about $100 million (FEER 1989a). Vietnam also ran up Asian Development Bank (ADB) arrears of $33.5 million (Indochina Chronology 1993b).

As a result of the American trade embargo, Vietnam primarily engaged in barter trade with the Soviet bloc for strategic goods; some 64 percent of SRV trade in 1988 was with the Soviet Union (Quinn-Judge and Hiebert 1988). Because the trade was unequal, with Vietnam receiving a greater value of imports than exports, Hanoi had to agree to place Soviet managers in charge of Vietnamese rubber plantations and similar enterprises. When the price of natural rubber increased in the mid-1980s, due to an increased demand for latex condoms and gloves in order to cope with the worldwide AIDS crisis, Hanoi derived little additional benefit and thus lusted to break free from economic dependence on Moscow. In short, the effect of the U.S. embargo was to force Vietnam away from reliance on the world market economy into the arms of the Soviet Union at a time when socialist countries in Eastern Europe were breaking free.

The American-sponsored embargo, however, had some holes: There was no specific ban on private investment by U.S. corporations for intra-Vietnam trade, though the Jackson–Vanik Amendment of 1974 prohibited aid to Communist countries, including investment guarantees; lack of diplomatic relations precluded bilateral economic agreements. Overseas Vietnamese sent money to their relatives in Vietnam through non-U.S. banks, thereby providing some $200 million in annual foreign exchange, mostly in the south (Hiebert 1989a).

Japan, meanwhile, continued to trade with Vietnam, obtaining raw materials of various sorts (Awanohara and Morrison 1989). Smuggling by Singaporean and other traders brought consumer goods to Vietnam, notably used motorbikes that Vietnamese purchased with U.S. dollars at government stores. Thai-manufactured products were sold openly in Vietnamese marketplaces, too. Despite the willingness of skilled Vietnamese workers to work at wages of about $10 per month (Indochina Digest 1994c), few foreign firms decided to profit from the situation, and the country manufactured few goods worth exporting.

In January 1987, the Congress of the Vietnamese Communist Party was aware that efforts to build socialism had failed, and the people were not economically satisfied with the regime (Pham and Le 2003). Reforms previously adopted in China were then instituted in Vietnam, though called "Hungarian reforms" in view of the hostile presence of the People's Liberation Army on Vietnam's northern border. The author of most Đổi Mới reforms, as they were called, was Nguyễn Xuân Oánh, former Prime Minister of South Vietnam, who had recently been elected to the SRV parliament. Rice farmers, who formerly grew a fixed amount for agricultural cooperatives in the form of yearly taxes, were now allowed to sell their surpluses on the open market. Soon, Vietnam became the third largest rice exporter (after Thailand and the United States). By 1988, about 60 percent of Vietnam's national income was derived from activity in the private sector (Quinn-Judge and Hiebert 1988).

The IMF then congratulated Vietnam for being the only country in the world to abolish dual exchange rates, end inflation, terminate perquisite salaries to government officials, and to end state subsidies to industry, which in turn had to buy and sell at market prices. The government accepted the world market rate for the đồng, the local currency, thereby abolishing the black market rate. The central bank stopped printing money unaccountably, and instead fully financed government from its revenues. For students, the most popular subject was business administration. Marxism, still required, was considered the most boring subject by students and faculty alike.

In 1988, after passage of a new investment law that provided liberal terms for foreign firms to operate in Vietnam, exports to Australia quadrupled compared to 1987 (Lincoln 1988). Honda announced a desire to establish a motorbike factory in Hồ Chí Minh City, but withdrew the offer under pressure from the American government (Hiebert 1988a). During 1989, forty-eight overseas investment projects, totaling nearly $500 million, were approved for joint ventures with business firms in Australia, Belgium, Czechoslovakia, France, India, Japan, the Netherlands, South Korea, the Soviet Union, Thailand, and the United Kingdom—but not the United States (Hiebert 1989b). For example, a consortium representing British Petroleum, Petrofina of Belgium, and Shell Oil Company signed a contract for exploration off the coast of Vietnam, while Mobil Oil and Standard Oil of California continued to await a lifting of the embargo to resume oil prospecting that they had conducted during the era of the former Republic of Vietnam. Desiring an IMF loan to create a foreign exchange reserve, Hanoi made a payment of $8.5 million on arrears dating from commitments made by the former government in Saigon (Chanda 1989). Despite pressure from the two American oil companies and other businesses, Washington blocked any such loan until 1993 (Hess 1988:154; Brown 2000:151).

During 1989, nevertheless, the U.S.-Vietnam Trade Council was formed and met for the first time. In accordance with the Road Map, to be discussed next, the U.S. Treasury Department permitted American banks to form arrangements with financial institutions already operating in Vietnam in February 1991, thereby facilitating the transfer of funds from Vietnamese Americans to their relatives in the homeland. Also in 1991, Washington allowed American businesses to open offices in Vietnam, starting 1992. The trade embargo finally ended in 1994, thanks to President Bill Clinton, who responded to domestic pressures after the 1993 election in Cambodia gave no cause for alarm that Vietnam was a threat in the region, though the arms embargo remained.

The "Road Map"

In August 1989, the USS *Ranger* rescued ten Vietnamese soldiers who were adrift from a barge that broke loose from its moorings during a storm near one of the Spratly Islands, showing that military cooperation on humanitarian matters was possible. But the highest levels in Washington still had not forgiven Vietnam for winning the war, and Hanoi had stopped expecting Washington to live up to the Paris Accord by providing aid for Vietnam's postwar reconstruction.

In late 1989, the international reaction to the American government's insistence on shoehorning the Khmer Rouge back to share power in Phnom Penh, which clearly caused the failure of the Paris Conference on Cambodia that year, was overwhelmingly negative (Haas 1991b:ch19–20). After the conference, Britain responded by resuming aid to Vietnam, France took steps to provide a loan, and Italy sent its foreign minister to normalize relations. Some members of Congress, furious over State Department obstructionism at Paris, demanded a change of policy.

In midsummer 1990, Secretary of State Baker rescinded the ban on official high-level contacts that had persisted since the war, and SRV diplomats were allowed to travel to discuss the MIA issue in Washington. In August, Baker met Foreign Minister Thạch at a hotel near the UN in New York. In April 1991, Assistant Secretary of State Richard Solomon announced a series of gradual steps toward normalization, known as the "road map." Vietnam's UN Ambassador Trịnh Xuân Lăng responded with four phases that led to normalization with the Socialist Republic of Vietnam (Pike 1994):

Phase I

The first phase was to go into effect immediately after Vietnam signed a peace agreement on Cambodia. In October 1991, when that agreement was signed by all parties, Baker kept the terms of the road map by announcing that SRV delegates to the UN, effective the day after Christmas, would be allowed to travel beyond the previous limit of twenty-five miles from New York. And the Treasury Department allowed American travel agencies to book and sell reservations for airfare and tours to Vietnam without a need for a special license.

In accordance with Phase I, Baker indicated that normalization talks could now begin, and newly assigned Foreign Minister Nguyễn Mẫn Cam went to Washington in October 1992 to open negotiations. Baker then stressed that progress on normalization talks depended on cooperation in resolving the MIA issue, yet another instance of moving the goal posts to delay normalization.

Phase II

The next crossroads on the "road map" was to be reached when a UN temporary authority for Cambodia, as agreed at the reconvened Paris Conference on Cambodia in 1991, began to supervise a ceasefire and demobilization of troops in Cambodia. During Phase II, certain elements of the trade embargo were to be lifted—commercial transactions for basic human needs (agriculture, medicines), communication links, and permission for American businesses to open offices in Vietnam in order to carry out feasibility studies and technical surveys and to sign but not implement contracts. France, which had been seeking since 1989 to provide a bridge loan among commercial banks of several countries in order to enable Hanoi to pay off its arrears to the IMF, was given the green light to do so by the U.S. government. The United States also indicated support for ADB and World Bank technical assistance projects. And a high-level delegation was to go to Hanoi for detailed normalization talks.

The starting date of the UN Transitional Authority for Cambodia (UNTAC) and thus of Phase II, was March 1992. In that month, Assistant Secretary of State Solomon went to Hanoi to begin normalization talks. In April, AT&T instituted direct dial service to and from Vietnam. In December, American businesses were allowed to negotiate and sign joint venture contracts, which would not go into effect until the trade embargo was lifted.

Phase III

The next part of the "road map" was to begin when UNTAC certified that no Vietnamese advisers or troops were in Cambodia, all Cambodian forces were in cantonments, and demobilization of all forces was proceeding. At this point, the SRV would be allowed to set up a Liaison Office in Washington, and the United States would have a similar office in Hanoi. The trade embargo was to be lifted, and the United States was to support loans for "basic human needs" projects to Vietnam.

Although UNTAC announced that there was no evidence of Vietnamese advisers or troops throughout 1992, the Khmer Rouge refused to place its troops in cantonments. Because Khmer Rouge actions were outside Hanoi's control, Washington allowed commercial transactions on "basic human needs" and waived licensing requirements for nongovernment aid organizations in April 1992. But the embargo otherwise remained, and Liaison Offices were not opened. The U.S. government thus enabled Khmer Rouge treachery to delay the "road map." Then in January 1993, Bush packed his bags and left Washington, and Bill Clinton's presidency began.

Instead of a Liaison Office, a "temporary" U.S. office opened at Hanoi in June 1991. The office expanded by early 1994 to include some twenty officials, including three mid-level Foreign Service officers and seventeen Defense Department employees or contract workers to investigate MIAs. In June, the two countries agreed to exchange diplomatic missions at the level of one rank below ambassador. Next, ambassadorial-rank James Hall was presented to Party Secretary-General Đỗ Mười as the head of the U.S. mission in Hanoi by Assistant Secretary of State Winston Lord in July. Housing and offices in Hanoi and Washington were needed to complete the agreement.

Phase IV

The end of the road was to be in sight when military demobilization was complete in Cambodia and elections in 1993 installed a new national assembly in Phnom Penh. On the day when the new Cambodian assembly opened, full diplomatic relations were to be restored, Washington would vote in favor of major Asian Development Bank, International Monetary Fund, and World Bank loans, and Vietnam was to receive consideration for most-favored-nation trading status.

When the Khmer Rouge refused to demobilize, that aspect of the Paris agreement was aborted. Cambodian elections were held in May 1993, and the new parliament convened in June.

With the authors of the "road map" no longer in power, President Clinton demurred on Vietnam after he took office to avoid the appearance of appeasing Hanoi. Efforts of Vietphobes to trump up evidence of MIAs slaughtered or still in captivity emerged at crucial times, prompting delays. However, during 1993 Washington did not object when several European countries and Japan arranged to clear Vietnam's ADB, IMF, and World Bank loan arrears. Hanoi also received aid commitments of nearly $2 billion from bilateral and multilateral sources (Indochina Chronology 1993a, 1993b; Hanoi Voice of Vietnam Network 1994).

Due to what Clinton termed "progress" on the MIA issue, the trade embargo finally was declared to end in February 1993, effective 1994, when he issued a waiver of the Jackson–Vanik Amendment that had proscribed trade with Communist countries, as noted above. By early May, forty-five countries had actively committed $9.1 billion in foreign investment; yet the United States ranked eighteenth, with only $78 million invested (Vietnam Economic

Times 1994). Vietnam planned to issue $2 billion in government bonds later in 1994 (Reuters 1994).

Beyond the "Road Map"

In March 1994, diplomatic normalization had been agreed to in principle, but Secretary of State Warren Christopher declared that Vietnam would have to do a great many things, including progress in human rights, before full normal relations would be established. In May, the new emissary to Hanoi clarified that "There is no road map" (Indochina Digest 1994a, 1994b). The goal posts, in short, had moved again.

With the endpoint of normalization still in doubt, negotiations proceeded on various issues. The fate of MIAs remained the most important issue. In response to the "road map," Hanoi gradually had been permitting more thorough inspections, and the United States responded each time by providing more humanitarian aid (FEER 1992). By 1994, there were about thirty U.S.–SRV joint missions to search for MIAs. The latest, which began in June 1994, involved 103 specialists for a period of 27 days, culminating in searches conducted at the hitherto secret base at Cam Ranh Bay (AP 1994). As of mid-1994, Vietnam had turned over 287 remains that were identified as Americans; the rest were unidentified (Esper 1994).

The two countries then discussed claims for diplomatic premises dating back to the war and other issues regarding the exchange of embassies. While discussing the possible text of a consular agreement, Hanoi balked in April 1994 on a proposed provision that would require SRV authorities to contact American officials within 72 hours in case an American, including a Vietnamese American, were detained in Vietnam (Wu 1994). Although the provision was in accordance with the Vienna Convention on Consular Relations of 1963, the problem was that Hanoi considered all persons of Vietnamese parentage to be citizens of Vietnam—that is, dual citizens. Whereas the SRV offered tax breaks to overseas Vietnamese in order to encourage investment, few were likely to take advantage as long they felt that they might be subject to the whims of Vietnam's judicial system without the protection of the American government. But Hanoi eventually agreed to the clause after more discussions between the two parties. Liaison Offices were installed in both capitals during 1994.

Then, twenty years after the United States pulled out of its embassy in Saigon, full diplomatic relations were finally established with Hanoi. Embassies opened in 1995, when both parties agreed to full normalization of diplomatic relations. Normalization of commercial relations was next on the agenda.

Among various economic issues, assets still needed to be un-frozen. According to Richard Newcomb, director of the U.S. Treasury Departments' Office of Foreign Assets Control, the amount involved was about $230 million, whereas Vietnam claimed $290 million (Pike 1994:17). Nevertheless, the former amount eventually was eventually disbursed.

Although American development aid to Hanoi was unlikely because of what the Clinton administration considered its poor human rights record, Vietnam was relieved when President Clinton decided to un-couple human rights from most-favored-nation status for China in mid-1994, which spilled over to Hanoi. Vietnamese exports were likely to be placed within the U.S. Generalized System of Preferences, exempt from tariffs, provided that Hanoi provided compensation for seized property of American citizens, according to U.S. law. Full economic normalization entailed the ability to secure Export–Import Bank credits, credit guarantees, and insurance for export shipments.

End of the Road

Subsequently, the United States and Vietnam signed a bilateral trade agreement in 2000 and a counter-narcotics Letter of Agreement in 2001. A bilateral Human Rights Dialog began in 2004 under the administration of President George W. Bush. In 2007, Congress approved Permanent Normal Trade Relations with Vietnam, though there was still a ban on arms sales due to human rights concerns.

In recent years, the U.S. Coast Guard has repeatedly protected Vietnamese fishing vessels from China (U.S. News & World Report 2012) as if the two countries were now allies—a reversal of American support for China in the Spratly Islands during 1988. And in 2013, the United States agreed to transfer nuclear fuel and technology to Vietnam to build its first nuclear power plant (Reuters 2013). The arms embargo that began in 1984 was relaxed in 2014 (BBC 2014) and abolished in 2016 by President Barack Obama as a final step in normalization of relations.

Hanoi has recently invited the United States to establish a presence at Cam Ranh Bay, not far from China's aggressive moves in the South China Sea. In March 2018, an American aircraft carrier was dispatched phoenix-like to the port of Danang, an eight-hour drive north of Cam Ranh Bay and much closer to Paracel Islands claimed by Vietnam (Mullany 2018). Exactly fifty years after the Tet Offensive, a de facto military alliance has quietly been established. Onetime enemies are now close friends.

Conclusion

Enemies in 1954, when Washington began to support a government in South Vietnam rather than insisting on a plebiscite that might have unified the country, the United States and Vietnam are now on friendly terms. As the superpower leading the West during the Cold War, Washington was reluctant to make any concessions to Communist countries and was upset when North Vietnamese troops showed up in Saigon during 1975 and then invaded Cambodia in 1978 and remained for almost eleven years in an alliance with the Soviet Union. And Brzezinski greenlighted China, without direct provocation, to attack Vietnam in 1979.

Nevertheless, diplomatic interaction occurred between the two countries because domestic pressures existed. Relatives of those who went missing in the war wanted answers, driving the early negotiations. Humanitarian agencies wanted to help, and oil companies sought entry to the Vietnamese economy. Senator John McCain also provided leadership.

Actions and negotiations on both sides went up and down (Chapter Appendix, Tables 3.1 and 3.2) until President Bill Clinton decided to finish the job. In short, negotiations began stiffly but became more conciliatory as they proceeded. With so many unilateral concessions, progress was assured, and the endgame was reached.

Commercial, diplomatic, and military relations between the United States and Vietnam proceed today as if nothing untoward had ever happened in the past. Yet the situation is quite different in the case of North Korea, as the following chapter recounts.

References

Albor, Teresa (1990). "Very Heavy Going: ODP Is Under Pressure to Solve Refugee Snarl," *Far Eastern Economic Review*, July 12: 55.

Aspen Institute (1988). *Recommendations for the New Administration on United States Policy Toward Indochina*. Queenstown, MD: Aspen Institute.

Associated Press (1994). "U.S. Vietnam Start New MIA Search," *Honolulu Advertiser*, June 17: E5.

Awanohara, Susumu, and Charles Morrison (1989). "Looking Beyond Cambodia: Japan and Vietnam," *Indochina Issues*, 89 (August).

Becker, Elizabeth (1986). *After the War Was Over: The Voices of Cambodia's Revolution and Its People*. New York: Simon & Schuster.

Belkin, Lisa (1988). "Children of 2 Lands in Search of Home," *New York Times*, May 19: 11.

Borg, Jim (1988). "Export: Agent Orange Not the Main Culprit in Forest Destruction," *Honolulu Star-Bulletin & Advertiser*, October 30: A5.

Brazaitis, Thomas J. (1989). "Viets Face Jail If They Arrange Vietnam Trips," *Honolulu Star-Bulletin*, May 26: A14.

British Broadcasting Corporation (2014). "US to Partially Lift Vietnam Arms Embargo," *bbc.com/news*, October 3.

Brown, Bob (1989). "Journey Brings Hope: Professor Learns Vietnamese Outlook," *Leader-Telegram* (Eau Claire, Wisconsin), January 31: 1–2A.

Brown, Frederick Z. (2000). "The United States and Vietnam." In *Honey and Vinegar: Incentives, Sanctions, and Foreign Policy*, eds. Richard N. Haass and Meghan L. O'Sullivan, Chapter 8. Washington, DC: Brookings.

Cerquone, Joseph (1989). "Visitation Rights," *Veteran*, September/October: 15.

Chanda, Nayan (1986). *Brother Enemy*. New York: Collier.

Chanda, Nayan (1989). "Rewards of Retreat: IMF and World Bank Prepare to Return to Vietnam," *Far Eastern Economic Review*, July 6: 52–53.

Chapon, Jean-Claude (1989). "Viet Ex-Prisoners, Kin to Be Resettled in U.S.," *Honolulu Advertiser*, July 31: A4.

Childress, Richard T., and Stephen J. Solarz (1998). "Vietnam: Detours on the Road to Normalization." In *Reversing Relations with Former Adversaries*, eds. C. Richard Nelson and Kenneth Weisbrode, Chapter 5. Gainesville: University of Florida Press.

Crossette, Barbara (1988). "Vietnamese Children of Americans Leave Thailand on Way to U.S.," *New York Times*, January 1: I–1,4.

Erlanger, Steven (1989). "U.S. Is Offered Offices in Vietnam for Gathering Data on the Missing," *New York Times*, November 17: A5.

Esper, George (1994). "War Veteran Named Top Hanoi Envoy," *Honolulu Advertiser*, July 3: A20.

Fadiman, Anne (1997). *The Spirit Catches You and You Fall Down*. New York: Farrar, Straus, Giroux.

Far Eastern Economic Review (1989a). "Aid Waits for Peace: Western Donor Countries in No Hurry to Help," *Far Eastern Economic Review*, April 22: 71.

Far Eastern Economic Review (1989b). "Discounting the Debt," *Far Eastern Economic Review*, May 11: 8.

Far Eastern Economic Review (1992). "Hanoi's MIA Moves Earn More U.S. Aid," *Far Eastern Economic Review*, March 19: 12.

Funseth, Robert L. (1989). *Orderly Departure of Refugees from Vietnam*. Washington, DC: U.S. Department of State, Current Policy No. 1199.

Goose, Stephen D., and R. Kyle Horst (1988). "Amerasians in Vietnam: Still Waiting," *Indochina Issues*, 80: 3.

Haas, Michael (1991a). *Cambodia, Pol Pot, and the United States*. New York: Praeger.

Haas, Michael (1991b). *Genocide by Proxy: Cambodian Pawn in a Superpower Chessboard*. New York: Praeger.

Hanoi International Service (1988). "Spokesman on Foreign Relations, Inmate Release," *Foreign Broadcast Information Service*, September 1: 56.

Hanoi Voice of Vietnam Network (1994). "Foreign Minister on 1993 Accomplishments," *Foreign Broadcast Information Service*, January 2: 37.

Hatfield, Larry D. (1990). "U.S. Veterans Returning to Vietnam as Peace Builders," *Honolulu Star-Bulletin*, September 5: A15.

Hess, Gary (1988). *Vietnam and the United States*. New York: Twayne.

Hiebert, Murray (1988a). "Foreign Investors Scramble for a Toehold," *Far Eastern Economic Review*, March 17: 22.

Hiebert, Murray (1988b). "Mixed Signals from Hanoi," *Far Eastern Economic Review*, November 17: 42–43.

Hiebert, Murray (1989a). "Converting to Trade: Foreign Business Lured by Potential Big Market," *Far Eastern Economic Review*, April 27: 73.

Hiebert, Murray (1989b). "The Toughest Battle: Vietnam Is Mobilizing International Resources to Salvage Its Economy," *Far Eastern Economic Review*, April 27: 69.

Honolulu Advertiser (1989a). "28 More Remains Reported," *Honolulu Advertiser*, June 16: A25.

Honolulu Advertiser (1989b). "U.S. Gets More Remains," *Honolulu Advertiser*, August 1: D1.

Honolulu Advertiser (1989c). "U.S. Giving Hanoi 'Aid'," *Honolulu Advertiser*, November 9: Dl.

Humeniuk, Bob (1988). "Shadowy Paymaster," *Far Eastern Economic Review*, October 13: 3.

Indochina Chronology (1992). *Indochina Chronology*, 11 (2): 7.

Indochina Chronology (1993a). *Indochina Chronology*, 12 (3): 5.

Indochina Chronology (1993b). *Indochina Chronology*, 12 (4): 3.

Indochina Digest (1994a). "Normal Ties with Vietnam Not Inevitable," *Indochina Digest*, 7 (May 27): 3.

Indochina Digest (1994b). "'Our Vietnamese Friends" *Indochina Digest*, 7 (March 11): 4.

Indochina Digest (1994c). "Rich Man, Poor Man," *Indochina Digest*, 7 (April 8): 3.

Institute of International Education (2010). "Top Places of Origin of International Students," Institute of International Education. www.iie.org/Research-and-Publications/Open-Doors/Data/International-Students/Leading-Places-of-Origin/2010-12.

Kaiser, Robert G. (2016). "The Disaster of Richard Nixon," *New York Review of Books*, 63 (7): 56ff.

King, Jessica (2012). "U.S. in First Effort to Clean up Agent Orange in Vietnam," cnn.com. Accessed August 10, 2015.

Klintworth, Gary (1989). *Vietnam's Intervention in Cambodia in International Law*. Canberra: Australian Government Publishing Service.

Lincoln, Ian (1988). Interview with the Australian ambassador to Vietnam, Hanoi, August 22.

Lindgren, Gören, G. Kenneth Wilson, and Peter Wallensteen (1989). "Armed Conflicts over Government and Territory." In *States in Armed Conflict*, ed. Peter Wallensteen, pp. 35–72. Report #30. Uppsala: Department of Peace and Conflict Research, University of Uppsala.

Logevall, Fredrik (2012). *Embers of War: The Fall of an Empire and the Making of America's Vietnam*. New York: Random House.

McAuliff, John (1989). Congressional testimony, May 1. Personal communication.

Minear, Larry (1988). "Private Aid and Public Policy: A Case Study," *Indochina Issues*, 82 (June): 4.

Moore, S. Jonathan (1990). "This Way Out: Amerasians Provide an Exit," *Far Eastern Economic Review*, July 12: 55.

Morse, Linda (1994). "Helping Hands," *Far Eastern Economic Review*, June 30: 4.

Mullany, Gerry (2018) "U.S. Plans to Send First Aircraft Carrier to Vietnam Since War's End," *New York Times*, January 25.

New York Times (1979). "Vietnam Links Withdrawal from Cambodia to China," *New York Times*, May 17: A5.

Oxfam America (1988). *Focus on Vietnam*. New York: Oxfam America.

Pham, Chi Do, and Duc Viet Le (2003). "A Decade of *Doi Moi* in Retrospect: 1989–99." In *The Vietnamese Economy*, eds. Binh Tran-Nam and Chi Do Pham, Chapter 41. New York: Routledge.

Pike, Douglas (1994). "Clinton Announces End of Nineteen Year Old Economic Embargo on Vietnam," *Indochina Chronology*, 13 (2): 16–17.

Quinn-Judge, Sophie, and Murray Hiebert (1988). "Ten Year Itch: Soviets Admit Much of Economic Aid to Hanoi Was Wasted," *Far Eastern Economic Review*, November 10: 23.

Reuters (1990). "Over 200 Vietnamese Return Home Voluntarily from Hong Kong," *GEnie*, August 9.

Reuters (1994). "Vietnam Plans to Make Debut on Capital Markets," *International Herald Tribune*, July 8: 15.

Reuters (2013). "U.S., Vietnam Sign Nuclear Trade Agreement," *Reuters*, October 10. www.reuters.com/article2013/10/10/us-usa-vietnam-nuclear-idUSBRE99904720131010. Accessed July 8, 2015.

Rosen, James (1992). "Russian: Viets Kept Some POWs: Says KGB Quizzed 3 of Them Years After the War Ended," *Honolulu Advertiser*, January 2: A1–2.

Small, Melvin Small, and J. David Singer (1982). *Resort to Arms: International and Civil Wars, 1916–1980*. Beverly Hills, CA: Sage.

United Kingdom, Foreign and Commonwealth Office (1988). "Soviet Bloc Aid to Special Friends," *Background Brief*, August: 5.

United Press International (1988). "U.S., Vietnam to Establish Amerasian Center in Vietnam," *GEnie*, December 2.

United States, Department of Commerce (1993). *1990 Census of Population: Asians and Pacific-Islanders*. Washington, DC: Government Printing Office.

United States, Senate, Committee on Foreign Relations (1977). *Report of the Presidential Commission on U.S. Missing and Unaccounted for in Southeast Asia*. Washington, DC: Government Printing Office.

U.S. News & World Report (2012). "U.S. Helps Vietnam Fishermen Who 'Get into Trouble' with China," *U.S. News & World Report*, April 9.

Vietnam Economic Times (1994). *Vietnam Economic Times*, 3 (June): 11.

Wu, Irene (1994). "Identity Crisis: U.S.–Hanoi Talks Stall on Foreign Nationality Issue," *Far Eastern Economic Review*, May 5: 32.

York, Geoffrey, and Hayley Mick (2008). "Last Ghost of the Vietnam War," *Globe and Mail*, July 12.

Yu, Alan K., Vladimir N. Pregelj, and Robert G. Suiter (1989). *Vietnam: Procedural and Jurisdictional Questions Regarding Possible Normalization of U.S. Diplomatic and Economic Relations*. Washington, DC: Congressional Research Service.

Appendix

Table 3.1. American Negotiations with Vietnam.

Year	Negative Moves	Year	Positive Moves
1954	USA begins trade embargo of NV	1968	USA begins peace negotiations
1956	USA refuses to allow elections in SV	1973	USA reaches peace agreement with V
1973	USA begins to refuse economic aid to V	1977	USA allows V planes to refuel in USA
1974	Jackson–Vanik Amendment (trade embargo)	1977	USA ends restrictions on travel to V
1975	USA begins trade embargo for all V	1977	US Postal Service accepts mail for V
1976	USA new precondition for negotiations: settle MIA problem	1977	USA votes for V membership in UN
1979	USA refuses to vote for UN peacekeepers in Cambodia	1977	USA begins back-channel talks with V
1979	USA OKs PRC attack on V	1977	USA sets up Commission on MIAs
1979	new USA precondition for negotiations: leave Cambodia	1979	USA sets up ODP
1979	USA disallows Amerasian emigrants	1981	Reagan allows children to send papers and pens to schoolchildren in V
1981	USA condemns V in Cambodia	1981	USA decreases restrictions on travel from V
1981	USA begins aid to troops opposing V	1984	USA allows Amerasians as immigrants
1982	ODP gridlock	1987	American Homecoming Bill passes

VIETNAM

Year	Negative Moves	Year	Positive Moves
1985	new USA precondition for negotiations: verified withdrawal from Cambodia	1987	Reagan appoints Vessey, who is diplomatic
1988	USA pressures Honda not to set up factory in V	1987	USA allows private economic aid to V
1989	USA disallows university study tour	1988	USA leases office in Hồ Chí Minh City
1989	USA false accusation on V re Cambodia	1989	USA accepts new office in Hanoi
1989	USA disallows French loan to V	1989	USA expands ODP
1992	new USA precondition for normalization: MIA issue resolved	1989	U.S.–V Trade Council formed
1994	new USA precondition for normalization: improvement in human rights	1989	U.S. military rescues V soldiers during storm
		1990	USA agrees to talk to V about Cambodia
		1990	USA OKs high-level diplomatic contact
		1991	USA allows remittances from Vietnamese Americans to go to banks in V
		1991	USA ends all restrictions on travel to V
		1991	USA proposes Road Map
		1991	USA allows V delegates at UN beyond New York
		1991	USA allows basic needs trade
		1991	USA allows French loan to V
		1992	USA allows basic needs loans
		1992	USA drops licensing requirement for private aid
		1992	USA allows V to open Washington office
		1992	USA OKs US businesses to have offices in V

(Continued)

Table 3.1. (*Continued*)

Year	Negative Moves	Year	Positive Moves
		1993	USA OKs technical assistance from Asian Development Bank and World Bank
		1993	USA allows loan of European countries + Japan to V
		1994	USA ends trade embargo of V except for arms
		1994	USA unfreezes V assets
		1995	USA–V full diplomatic normalization
		2000	US–V trade agreement
		2014	arms embargo ended

Table 3.2. Vietnamese Negotiations with the United States.

Year	Negative Moves	Year	Positive Moves
1954	NV begins to aid insurgents in SV	1968	V agrees to negotiate with USA for peace
1976	unification of V	1978	V drops economic aid precondition for talks
1977	NV: economic aid is precondition for talks	1979	V agrees to ODP
1984	V suspends ODP cooperation	1985	V returns MIAs
1986	V reimposes aid precondition for talks	1985	V allows excavation for MIAs
1986	V suspends ODP cooperation	1985	V promises to resolve MIA issue by 1987
1987	V imposes conditions on release of political prisoners	1985	V offers to leave Cambodia by 1990
1988	V suspends MIA search	1987	V agrees to broader ODP
1994	V opposes Vienna Convention guarantee	1987	V drops economic aid precondition
1994	V wants a larger amount of assets unfrozen than Washington will allow	1987	V allows forensic personnel to find MIAs

Year	Negative Moves	Year	Positive Moves
		1988	V rescinds MIA search suspension
		1988	V allows U.S. office in Hồ Chí Minh City
		1988	V allows MIA search all over the country
		1988	V offers USA to open 15 offices in country
		1988	V withdraws all advisers from Cambodia
		1988	first V discussion about boat people
		1989	V agrees to plan for boat people
		1989	V withdraws all troops from Cambodia
		1989	V makes many concessions at Paris talks
		1989	V allows more exit visas in ODP
		1989	V drops preconditions for release of political prisoners
		1991	V accepts the Road Map
		1992	V allows a U.S. office in Hanoi
		1994	V increases MIA efforts
		1994	V concedes Vienna Convention guarantee
		1994	V accepts Washington's asset unfreezing figure
		2000	V agrees to a trade agreement with USA

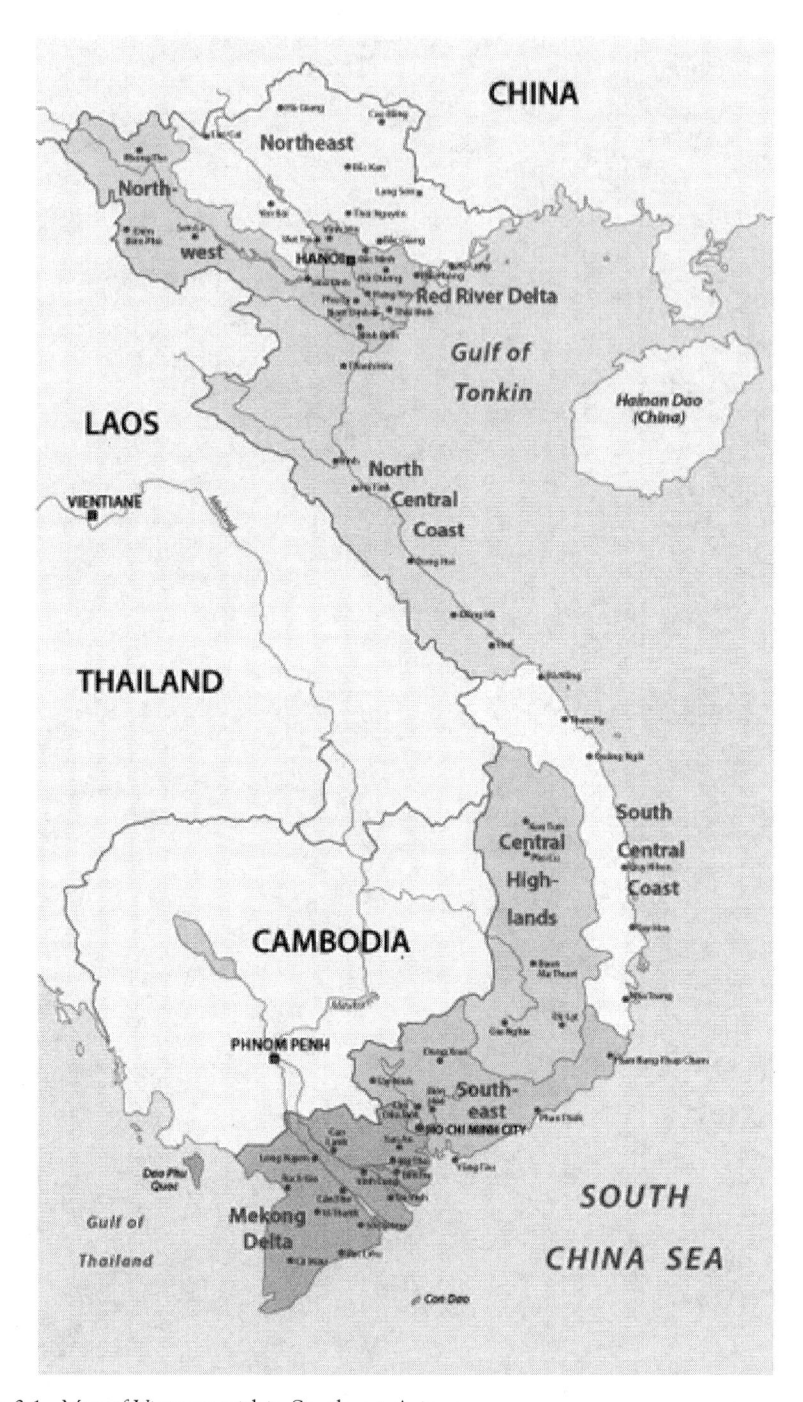

Figure 3.1. Map of Vietnam within Southeast Asia.

Figure 3.2. Skyline of Hanoi, Vietnam.

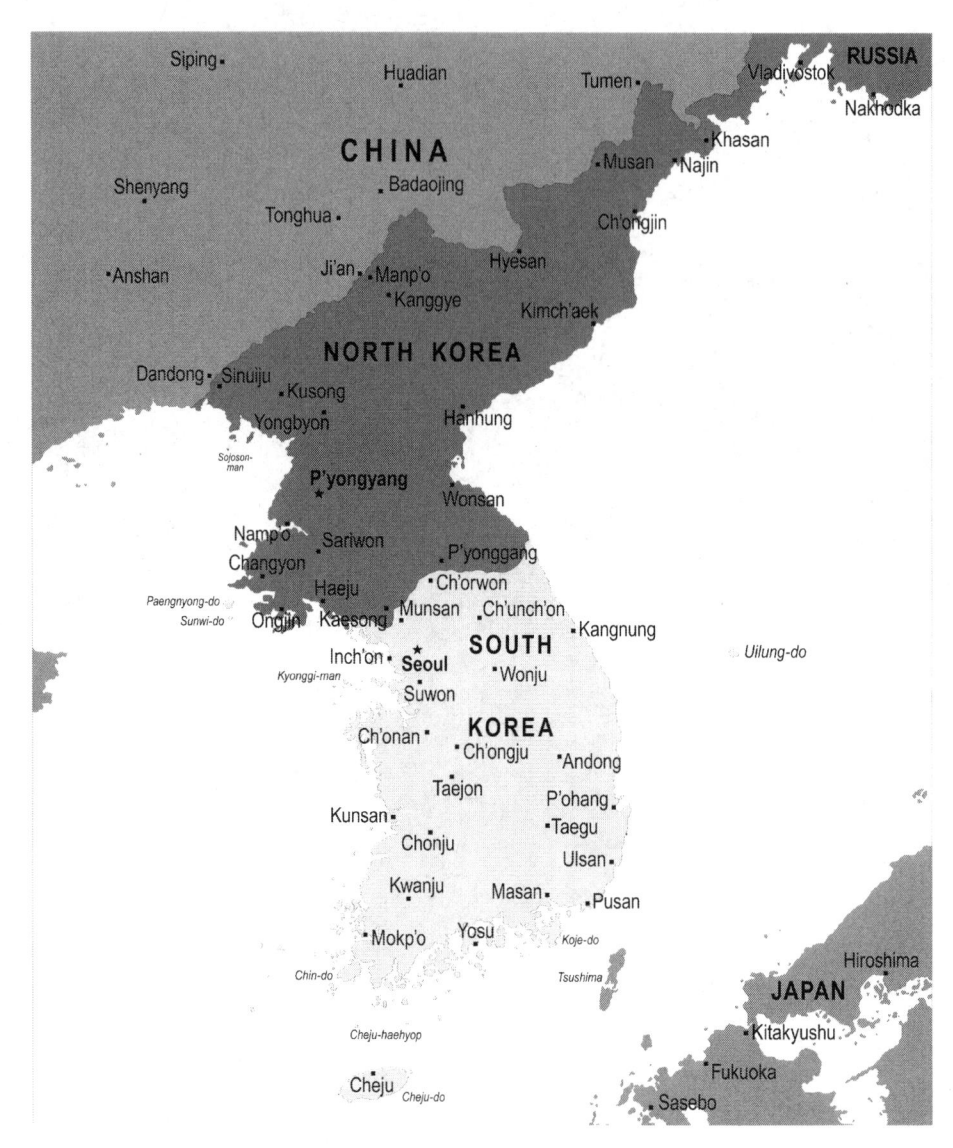

Figure 3.3. Map of Korea within Northeast Asia.

Figure 3.4. Skyline of Seoul, South Korea.

Figure 3.5. Skyline of Pyongyang, North Korea.

· 4 ·

NORTH KOREA

Similar to Vietnam, the Korean peninsula began World War II as a colony of a major power. Japan had ruled Korea since 1910, so the United States was a de facto ally of Kim Il Sung, who later was the leader of North Korea. At the very end of the war, American and Soviet troops entered the country. At the Moscow Conference in December 27, 1945, the Soviet Union and the United States agreed to divide the peninsula into north and south zones, with a temporary division at the 38th parallel. Delegates of the two countries met at Seoul in early 1946 to set up the USA–USSR Joint Commission. But the two countries disagreed on how to proceed.

In 1947, the UN General Assembly called for elections throughout the country to establish a provisional government that would draw up a constitution. The following year, the United Nations established the UN Commission for Unification and Rehabilitation of Korea, whereupon Soviet troops withdrew from the North, though American forces remained in the South, where a Republic of Korea (ROK) was formed. Kim Il Sung formed the Democratic People's Republic of Korea (DPRK) in the North, applied for admission to the UN, and organized the Democratic Front for the Reunification of the Fatherland, consisting of political parties and social organizations on both sides of the 38th parallel to call for unification of the peninsula.

Lacking consensus between the DPRK and the American-occupied south, war broke out on June 25, 1950. The UN Security Council met that day, demanding withdrawal of DPRK troops to positions north of the 38th parallel. A sizeable increase in American troops was then committed to defend the ROK on June 30. On July 14, the United Nations Command was authorized to defend the southern part of the country. General Douglas MacArthur, who had been in charge of the Allied occupation of Japan, was accepted as the head of the UN Command.

At first, North Korean troops nearly won, encircling the area around Busan. When American forces entered, the direction shifted northward almost to the border with China, whereupon India withdrew support from the UN Command. Chinese troops then sent "human waves" into the conflict, and the battle lines stabilized about halfway down the peninsula.

The war continued until the Korean War Armistice Agreement, negotiated over about two years, was signed on July 27, 1953. The agreement set up a demilitarized zone 2,200 yards centered around the 38th parallel. In addition, the truce established a Neutral Nations Supervisory Commission (NNSC) and a Military Armistice Commission (MAC); the latter was to consist of one delegate from the DPRK and one from the UN Command, with the Republic of Korea as an observer. NNSC had responsibility for investigating armistice violations. MAC, which was to meet at the border in Panmunjom, had the dual responsibility of resolving complaints regarding armistice violations and of negotiating the armistice agreement into a peace agreement. Signatories to the armistice were the Korean People's Army, the Chinese People's Volunteers, and the UN Command—an agreement between military forces rather than governments. The agreement was officially adopted by the UN General Assembly. South Korea and the United States refused to accept the truce, so they are technically still at war with North Korea. Two months after the agreement, Seoul and Washington signed a mutual defense agreement, and American troops remained in the South. Chinese military forces departed in 1958.

In 1954, both Korean governments were represented at the Geneva conference on Indochina, hoping to go beyond the armistice to have their views adopted. South Korea proposed that UN-supervised elections should be held in the country, Chinese forces should withdraw, and UN peacekeepers should maintain the ceasefire. North Korea countered that the UN should insist that foreign (American and Chinese) forces should leave the country and then sponsor elections to be run by an all-Korean commission throughout the entire country. Both China and the Soviet Union urged negotiations toward unification of the country. None of the proposals was accepted (Bailey 1992:163, 167–68).

Initially, NNSC was composed of teams from Czechoslovakia and Poland in the northern demilitarized zone (DMZ), with Sweden, and Switzerland having offices in the southern DMZ. Operations of the NNSC were hampered by the fact that both North and South Korea wanted to increase their forces and demanded that NNSC stop inspecting. Accordingly, NNSC stopped investigations, recorded troop levels annually, and registered complaints from both sides. The DPRK expelled the Czech Republic representative in 1993 and Poland's official was asked to leave in 1995, leaving the remaining two countries with the same assignment as before, though Poland rejoined in 2008 on the South Korean territory. Ever since, NNSC has sought to aid communications between the parties.

No peace agreement has ever emerged. South Korean President Syngman Rhee opposed armistice negotiations and refused to sign the agreement. Instead of the United States as a party to the armistice, the UN Command signed on the dotted line. North Korea has been increasingly frustrated that there is no peace agreement and that the Democratic People's Republic of Korea does not have normal relations with either Republic of Korea or the United States. Were both Koreas and the United States to sign a peace treaty together, their representatives would have to ask permission from the United Nations to supersede the armistice agreement. Over the years, leaders of the two Koreas have met and proposed reunification plans (Haas 1989:App; 2012:App), but they have never been implemented.

After the end of the Cold War, North Korea permitted South Koreans to visit the North, and South Korean businesses were allowed to establish factories in the north. But, as noted below, relations have fluctuated from mostly hostile to occasionally friendly between the two Korean governments over the years (ibid., ch2).

The key to resolving the intra-Korean conflict would be a normalization of relations between Pyongyang and Washington, which is the focus of the present chapter. Some parallels with the United States–Vietnam normalization process begin the discussion:

"Healing the Wounds of War"

Although the armistice agreement had no provision about "healing the wounds of war," some 205,000 prisoners of war (POWs) were exchanged on both sides within sixty days after the signing of the armistice agreement (Steuck 1995:216). Neither side held back prisoners. About one British soldier, 21 American military personnel, and 327 South Korean soldiers preferred to stay in North Korea, prompting the charge that they were "brainwashed." Except for a committed Marxist, the rest of the Americans traveled to Eastern Europe and eventually left the Communist bloc. In addition, some 22,000 Chinese and North Korean POWs refused to go home (Wikipedia 2017:2).

American war deaths were 36,914, about the same as in Vietnam (CBS 2000). Others killed were 58,127 South Koreans, 215,000 North Koreans, and 114,000 Chinese, 315 from the Soviet Union, and smaller numbers for other countries fighting under the UN Command—Australia, Belgium, Canada, Colombia, Ethiopia, France, Netherlands, Philippines, South Africa, Thailand, and Turkey.

In 1954, North Korea launched Operation Glory to locate soldiers missing in action (MIAs), soon returning about 3,000 American bodies (DPAA 2017). Estimates are that at least 5,300 American soldiers are still missing (ibid.; Kramer 1994; U.S. National Guard 2017). Despite meetings at Panmunjom for decades, both Pyongyang and Washington devoted very little attention to the matter despite conducting 33 search operations. Without any interest in deriving bargaining leverage, North Korea returned 208 boxes of MIA remains from 1990 to 1994 (CNN 2017). From 1996, the 220 more sets of remains were located by American personnel conducting search operations north of the 38th parallel. The search stopped in 1995, when the Clinton administration was criticized for paying for each body. After 2005, despite finding 87 more bodies since 1996, the United States refused to negotiate over the issue, though the DPRK has been ready to return an additional 120 sets of remains, and Coalition of Families of Korean and Cold War POW/MIAs pressed the American government to proceed (U.S. National Guard 2017). Bill Richardson helped with 6 more remains in 2007. After North Korea raised the issue in 2016, the matter was raised at the Singapore Summit in 2018, and progress is expected.

North and South Korea suffered much damage in the war, but no promise for humanitarian aid was made in the armistice agreement. Washington never pledged to provide reconstruction aid to the North, which similarly never offered funds to the South for war damage. American aid has instead gone to the South.

Under the terms of the Trading with the Enemy Act of 1917, trade with North Korea was banned during the 1950s. President Jimmy Carter cut all military aid to the South by 1978, though his adviser Zbigniew Brzezinksi successfully advised him not to carry out his campaign pledge to remove all American troops (Cummings 2005:475).

North Korea, meanwhile, adopted the *chuch'e* ideology, which meant a commitment to self-reliance, including a refusal to rely on any single country for economic assistance or trade. Some $600 million in loans from European and Japanese banks in the 1970s remained largely unpaid at the end of the 1980s (FEER 1989). North Korea's economy was initially superior to that in the South, but the situation reversed by the 1970s.

North Korean secretiveness about conditions of ordinary citizens has meant that American and Western journalists and scholars could travel to the showcase city of Pyongyang, but trips to the countryside have largely been forbidden. Some visitors were allowed in the mid-1970s, but travel was soon stopped and then resumed in 1987. Citizen travel out of North Korea to the United States, which began in 1989, was largely limited to attendance by scholars at professional meetings. In 2008, nevertheless, the New York Philharmonic Orchestra performed in North Korea. Washington banned all travel to North Korea in 2017, when the two countries saber-rattled each other.

North Korean citizens have received remittances from relatives in Japan, estimated in 1994 at $60 million annually (Smith 1994), but not from the United States, where North Koreans evidently never moved. Instead, North Korean defectors have resettled in South Korea. Seoul began to trade with the North via Hongkong in the 1980s, whereupon the U.S. relaxed the embargo with the North, though restrictions were tightened later.

In the 1990s, when a famine caused an estimated three million deaths (Collins 2014:4), North Korea adopted economic reforms along the lines of China, but foreign investment has been limited. Since the North did not apply for membership in the Asian Development Bank, the International Monetary Fund, or the World Bank, multilateral loans were not on the DPRK shopping list.

UN-authorized economic sanctions, first imposed in 1993, have remained. Food grains, in the form of 240,000 tons (mostly of biscuits), were sent from the United States in 2009, when North Korea re-invited nuclear weapons inspectors, but the aid ended after Pyongyang tried to launch a satellite later that year (Eckert 2012).

An estimate in 1994 was that $600 billion was the minimum required to bring North Korea up to the level of the South (Bowring 1994). Then and now, there have been no prospects for development aid anywhere near that level.

In short, "wounds of war" have not been an issue between Pyongyang and Washington. The problem between the two countries is that there has been mutual hostility and thus neither a peace treaty nor normalization of relations.

Signs of the Continuation of the War

Prospects for war on the peninsula remain. Troops on both sides of the DMZ are poised for any contingency. Since 1955, forces of South Korea and the United States have conducted joint military exercises, causing North Korea to fear that they are preparing for an invasion of the North. Each time exercises are planned, the UN Command is informed and then conveys the information to the North Korean People's Army in advance, assuring Pyongyang that the exercises aim to demonstrate defensive capabilities. The Neutral Nations Supervisory Commission then monitors the exercises to ensure that there are no violations of the armistice agreement, such as the introduction of new weapons systems.

Four phases of military exercises have been held (Collins 2014), each time protested by North Korea as preparatory to an invasion. The earliest phase [1955] consisted of two exercises to ensure that the two forces were satisfactorily coordinated. The "Second Korean War" phase [1966–1975] occurred after North Korea engaged in armed infiltration operations in which 75 American soldiers were killed and 111 wounded, while more than 1,000 South Korean military and police died along with 171 civilians, and 300 North Koreans were killed inside South Korea. During the "expanded capabilities" phase [1976–1991], the exercise grew from 100,000 to 200,000 troops, while the North Korean army rose to over one million on active duty. North Korean leader Kim Il Sung was reportedly terrified by the capabilities demonstrated during the annual exercise (Farrell 2009). Due to North Korea's efforts to develop nuclear and missile capabilities from 1992, the current era is known as the "asymmetric capabilities" phase. But just when negotiations looked promising, as noted below, the exercises were cancelled.

The DPRK has strenuously objected to the military exercises. Accordingly, their armed forces have held their own maneuvers. In 2017, they lined up along the coastline in the largest demonstration ever (Maja 2017).

The armistice agreement provided that no new weapons could be introduced except to replace existing arsenals on a piece-by-piece basis. American nuclear weapons were introduced in South Korea during 1958, deliberately violating paragraph 13(d) of the armistice agreement (Selden and So 2004; Lee 2008). Although the United States tried to justify the action in response to a violation by North Korea, no evidence was presented to support that claim, evidently to avoid giving the DPRK fuel for propaganda (USDS 1957). Pyongyang then denounced the violation, dug massive underground fortifications, and moved conventional forces along the DMZ. In 1961, Pyongyang signed defense agreements with Beijing and Moscow. Although they asked both countries two years later for help to develop nuclear weapons, their request was turned down (Selden and So 2004:77–80).

In 1964, U.S. military dropped leaflets on North Korea containing a "safe conduct pass" to encourage defections (Friedman 2013; U.S. Air Force 1979). But the campaign was abandoned in 1968.

In 1968, the North Korean Navy seized the USS *Pueblo* and held the crew hostage. Although the crew was released after eleven months of negotiations, the ship was retained by the DPRK. The following year, North Korea shot down an American reconnaissance airplane. In response, the United States denounced the attack, increased troops in South Korea, but limited further spy flights, relying as before on satellite photography. Relations calmed down after President Richard Nixon removed one-third of American troops from South Korea shortly after taking office in 1969. Dialog between North and South Korea over reunification began in 1972, the first positive sign in their relations. Leaders of both countries then met together. As a result, the DPRK was diplomatically recognized throughout the world, including within parts of the UN system. In 1974, North Korea proposed a peace treaty, but found no interlocutors.

During the presidential election of 1976, candidate Jimmy Carter promised to withdraw American forces from South Korea. In office, he failed to do so, sending the first concrete signal to North Korea that American leaders do not always keep their promises. An opportunity for détente was missed as a result.

The détente between the United States and China during the 1970s caused Pyongyang to become more reliant on Moscow, which in the early 1980s responded to North Korea's request for assistance in expanding the power grid by helping to plan for a nuclear power plant at Yongbyon. But both China and Russia refused to help North Korea develop nuclear weapons. Soviet aid to North Korea ended during the perestroika era of the late 1980s.

In 1988, Washington put DPRK on the list of state sponsors of terrorism. The move, with direct implications for sanctions, was the culmination of several actions by North Korea, including shipping goods to other state sponsors of terrorism, the bombing of a South Korean airplane in 1987, and kidnapping of Japanese inside Japan over the years (Martin 2008:83).

The collapse of the Soviet Union in 1991 made North Korea turn toward China again. In the spirit of the post-Cold War era, both North and South Korea were allowed to join the United Nations as separate countries that year. In 1992, China normalized relations with South Korea, whereupon neither Beijing nor Pyongyang engaged in serious diplomatic exchanges with each other for the next seven years (Chen 2003:9). At some point, feeling isolated, Pyongyang decided to develop a nuclear deterrent.

In 1994, the United States deployed Patriot missiles in South Korea. The DPRK considered that the armistice agreement of 1953 had thereby been terminated and pulled out of the Military Armistice Commission while still promising to continue contact at Panmunjom and to observe the armistice (BBC 2013). An American helicopter was shot down in December 1994 while straying accidentally into North Korean airspace. The pilot was released thirteen days later; the helicopter co-pilot, however, was killed when shot down (Greenhouse 1994). In 2009, Pyongyang bombarded Yeonpeong, a contested island where South Koreans had taken residence (BBC 2009). In 2010, North Korea sank a South Korean patrol vessel.

Although North Korea later developed nuclear weapons and has made threats related to their arsenal, often echoed by the United States, most experts agree that Pyongyang's foreign policy has been entirely rational (Fisher 2016), following the playbook of deterrence theory. Pyongyang is unlikely to surrender its nuclear capacity or otherwise to disclose its true military potential, so long as there is a fear of a reckless attack led by the United States.

The South Korea Tango

Although Vietnam's interlude in Cambodia stopped prospects for normalization with both countries during the 1980s, relations between Seoul and Washington have continued on a positive basis without interruption. However, South Korea has undergone many political changes, including the rise and fall of five republican constitutions and a dozen presidents. The country was finally stabilized in 1987, thanks to a democratic protest that led the following year to the establishment of the current Sixth Republic. During the 1988 Olympic Games, Seoul might have allowed some sporting events to be held in Pyongyang, but Cold War diplomacy by the North was less than shrewd (Radchenko 2011). The DPRK's unyielding demands for one-third of the games were not accepted by the International Olympic Committee, and North Korea boycotted the games.

South Korean policies toward North Korea have been mostly hostile over the years. Syngman Rhee, president from 1946 to 1960, was arguably the most hostile: He refused to sign the armistice, preferring unification under his rule. The goal of one Korea has been written into the various South Korean constitutions.

Seoul and Washington formed a mutual defense pact in 1953. Ever since, American troops have remained in South Korea. Pyongyang would like the troops removed, but American forces will remain as long as the United States prefers to consider North Korea an adversary; the strategic location is of such importance to the Pentagon that American leaders have never supported peaceful demilitarization of the peninsula.

Some of the twists and turns of American policy toward North Korea have occurred in consultation with South Korea presidents. Although the two Korean leaders signed a peninsula-wide denuclearization pledge in 1992, a major breakthrough came late in 1998 with the election of Kim Dae Jung, whose "Sunshine Policy" allowed South Korean tourists to visit an important destination in the North, while South Koreans were able to visit relatives in the North, and joint business enterprises were established. At the 2004 Summer Olympics in Athens, the two Koreas marched together in the opening ceremony but competed separately; the same was true in the 2006 Winter Olympics in Turin, Italy. For his efforts, Kim was awarded the Nobel Peace Prize. His successor, Roh Moo Hyun, continued the same policies during his term, which ended in 2008.

For the next decade, South Korean presidents maintained the traditional policy of opposition to Pyongyang. A more confrontational policy returned with the election of President Lee Myung Bak, and verbal hostility toward the North increased during the tenure of the next president, Park Geun Hye, from 2013 to 2017. As a result, North Korea discontinued the hotline and other cooperation measures with the South.

However, Moon Jae In's election in 2017 signaled that dialog would be more likely; he knew that common language alone would facilitate dialog, and he did not want to subcontract the peace of the peninsula to someone as verbally reckless as Donald Trump, whom he pointedly urged to avoid war (Choe 2017; Stiles 2017). Trump distanced himself from South Korea first by threatening to end a bilateral trade agreement and later by placing a tariff on steel made in the ROK. As indicated in developments cited below, Moon indicated that he would seek to establish a continuing dialog with North Korea. His goal was to restore some of the cooperative ventures that were discontinued in response to his predecessor's harsh rhetoric, and to work toward denucleariztion and the possibility of a permanent peace (Stiles 2018a), something that the United States never put on the agenda during decades of confrontation and diplomatic failure until the Singapore Summit between Donald Trump and Kim Jong Un in June 2018.

Route to a "Road Map"

Efforts to forge an agreement between North Korea and the United States have encountered many hurdles. Based on information from the Arms Control Association and other sources, the following timeline of events reveals that the administration President Bill Clinton from 1993 to 2001 made more headway than any other president and nearly brought about normalization of relations to counter the DPRK's incipient efforts to develop nuclear weapons:

The negotiation narrative begins in 1983, when Pyongyang offered to abandon development of a nuclear power facility if Washington would agree to normalize relations, but the Reagan administration passed up the opportunity. Soviet aid to North Korea ended in 1985, whereupon Beijing became Pyongyang's best friend. Even so, under Soviet pressure (Kerr 2005:421), North Korea acceded to the Nuclear Non-Proliferation Treaty (NPT) that year and admitted inspectors of the International Atomic Energy Agency (IAEA). Pyongyang, however, did not complete the safeguards agreement with IAEA, demanding that the withdrawal of American nuclear weapons from South Korea must come first. In 1984, the DPRK tested Soviet-type low-range Scud-B missiles six times, three of which failed but did not do so again until 1990.

IAEA was blocked from entry in early 1986 to protest the annual military exercises between South Korea and the United States, but they were allowed back when the exercises concluded later that year. By 1989, IAEA inspectors deemed North Korea in compliance with the NPT.

The Cold War began to wane in 1989, when the Berlin Wall fell. More missile tests were held in 1990 and 1991. They may have given some sense of deterrent capability, but not much.

When the Soviet Union collapsed in 1991, North Korea turned toward China for support. But Beijing did not respond for the next seven years. Without an ally, North Korea decided to develop nuclear weapons and missile technology as a way to deter the United States while developing foreign exchange through missile and weapons sales.

In 1991, as a sign of the end of the Cold War, the two Koreas signed a Joint Declaration on Denuclearization, and the United States withdrew all nuclear weapons on land and sea from the Korean peninsula and surrounding waters (cf. Kristensen 2005). Although Pyongyang signed the IAEA safeguards agreement and admitted inspectors in 1992, Washington imposed sanctions on two North Korean corporations for selling missile technology to Pakistan. The UN followed suit in 1993 after Pyongyang expressed displeasure over the annual military exercises between American and South Korean military forces by refusing entry to IAEA inspectors and threatened withdrawal from NPT.

Because of apparent discrepancies in the DPRK report on compliance, IAEA inspectors requested another visit in 1992. But North Korea refused in early 1993, once again objecting to the projected annual joint military exercises between South Korea and the United States, but now also threatening to withdraw from NPT.

When DPRK missiles were launched in 1993, Iranians and Pakistanis were present. Clearly, they were interested buyers (CBS 2017).

In June 1993, after U.S. intelligence photos indicated something suspicious, the United States engaged in back-channel talks with the North at the UN headquarters in New York, fearing that the DPRK might develop nuclear weapons. Bilateral talks at the UN on two occasions resulted in an American assurance against the threat and use of force as well as a promise not to interfere with North Korean internal affairs. DPRK negotiators then made an offer similar to the one in 1983—normalization in exchange for abandonment of its nuclear program. North Korea also withdrew the threat to leave NPT, and agreed to allow IAEA inspections. In the resulting Joint Statement, the United States agreed to negotiate so that the North could buy and learn to operate a light-water reactor in order to replace its nuclear reactor and to discuss the possibility of economic and political normalization.

But the United States insisted on inspections before talks on normalization, visibly frustrating North Korean negotiators. Instead, Washington decided to develop a national defense system (NDS) for South Korea as a signal to Pyongyang that the nuclear threat might be countered in the future (Lindsay and O'Hannon 2001).

In early 1994, Pyongyang allowed IAEA inspectors to visit. The inspectors confirmed that rods of spent nuclear fuel had been removed from the reactor core, though they were placed in a cooling pond, where their plutonium could later be extracted, but not while IAEA was present, as previously agreed. Subsequently, when the United States did not begin normalization talks as promised, North Korea threatened to pull out of IAEA, though not NPT, and re-fueled the Yongbyon reactor, provoking a crisis.

Washington was intent on stopping the development of nuclear weapons, and even mentioned the option of launching war (Sigal 1998:70; Litwak 2000:111), though North Korea's overall military capabilities deterred that option (Kang 2003:320). Moreover, as David Kang has argued persuasively, Washington realized that Pyongyang could have smuggled nuclear weapons into the United States but failed to do so because nuclear weapons development was being used as a bargaining chip to seek normalization. As Peter Howard (2004:811) has reframed the narrative, the balance of threats had superseded old-fashioned balance-of-power thinking as the basis for deterrence.

In June 1994, former President Jimmy Carter accepted an invitation from Kim Il Sung to open a dialog that would put all issues on the negotiating table. Pyongyang then indicated willingness to suspend construction of a 50-megawatt plutonium reactor in exchange for heating oil and other energy aid, including a light-water reactor to replace the graphite nuclear reactor.

Agreed Framework

North Korea proved willing to make a deal. After months of negotiations, both sides adopted the Agreed Framework in October 1994, an instrument designed as a "road map" leading toward normalization, with four components or sections:

Section 1

Under the first element of the Agreed Framework, Washington promised to supply light-water reactors (Lauren, Craig, George 2007) and never to use nuclear weapons against the North (Pollack 2003:18). North Korea, in turn, agreed to abandon work on its nuclear reactor. In accordance with the loosely worded agreement, Pyongyang asked Washington to normalize relations in exchange for permission to allow full inspection of nuclear facilities. The United States insisted on inspection before talks on normalization, and the

DPRK accepted that condition. The light-water reactors were to be supplied by an international consortium, soon known as the Korean Energy Development Organization (KEDO).

Section 2

The next element was to provide heavy fuel oil to North Korea for electricity generation. The special oil shipment was to be a reward for Pyongyang's cooperation during 1995 in storing spent fuel so that none could be used to develop nuclear weapons. The canning of all accessible spent fuel rods and rod fragments was to be completed by 2005. In return, the United States promised "full normalization of political and economic relations."

Section 3

North Korea agreed to freeze all nuclear activity and allow IAEA monitoring. Upon completion of the light-water reactor, Pyongyang would dismantle the nuclear program and expel all spent rods from the country.

Section 4

North Korea pledged to remain in the NPT and to continue allowing IAEA inspectors. After a significant portion of the light-water reactor was completed, but before destruction of nuclear components, Pyongyang pledged to admit past violations to IAEA.

Signing of the Agreed Framework was considered a major breakthrough and explicitly reaffirmed by the Joint Declaration of 1991 and Joint Statement of 1993. IAEA soon confirmed that the Yongbyon reactor and all three DPRK nuclear facilities were no longer operational. To show good faith, the United States cancelled joint military exercises with South Korea in 1994 and 1995, and North Korea was removed from Washington's list of "rogue states" in 1996. The framework was scheduled to run several years, giving Washington an opportunity to become accustomed to negotiating with North Korea, whereupon normalization talks would occur.

But in December, the DPRK military shot down an American helicopter that strayed into North Korean territory. The United States contemplated military retaliation until Congressional representative Bill Richardson was dispatched to Pyongyang for negotiations. The incident was due to pilot error during a training mission, and Richardson eased the situation. The Agreed Framework was then put back on track.

KEDO was founded in 1995, with Japan and South Korea as additional members, which could readily travel to the site to handle engineering requirements, such as how deep to dredge the harbor for unloading of shipments (Howard 2004:818). But the American military exercises with South Korea resumed in 1996, suspecting cheating by North Korea in freezing the nuclear program. Both countries felt betrayed.

The Clinton administration underestimated Pyongyang's impatience about normalization of relations. Lacking financing from Congress as well as Japan and South Korea, KEDO took longer than Washington promised, with no contract signed until 2000, and no site construction until 2001, though $2.5 million was later raised from thirty countries (KEDO 2006). The project was "suspended" in 2003. North Korea, meanwhile, presumed that the United States was not abiding by the Agreement when fuel oil shipments were delayed and rarely arrived on time; amounting to $500 million over the years (Manyin and Nikitin 2004), they were stopped in 2002, when North Korea was suspected of resuming uranium enrichment (Howard 2004:818). Moreover, KEDO employed many non-Korean workers, depriving Pyongyang of the opportunity to earn hard currency (ibid., 820). And normalization talks were never held. Both sides blamed each other.

Talks on Missile Proliferation and Sales

Nuclear technology issues could not be separated from the issue of missile development and proliferation. North Korean businesses, for example, had sold missiles to Iran for foreign exchange. Carter and Kim also agreed to separate talks on missile development, in 1996, after Pyongyang suspended construction of a 50-megawatt plutonium reactor. There were eight rounds of talks on the matter:

Round 1 (April 21–22, 1996)

In initial statements, the United States asked North Korea to adhere to the Missile Technology Control Regime, a voluntary agreement to control ballistic missiles sales. DPRK requested compensation for the loss of revenue that would result from compliance with the regime. No agreement was reached.

Meanwhile, on a dare, American Evan Hunziker swam across the Yalu River to North Korea in August. Arrested as a spy, he was the first American ever arrested by the DPRK. A few weeks later, a North Korean submarine full of commandos landed on South Korean soil, something that the military realized was a mistake amid the missile talks. Two months after his detention, Hunziker was released with the aid of Congressional Representative Bill Richardson, who accompanied a State Department delegation.

Round 2 (June 11–12, 1997)

The positions stated during Round 1 were reaffirmed, again without an agreement. Then in August 1997 and April 1998, the United States imposed sanctions for unspecified missile proliferation activities. The Korean Central News Agency responded that DPRK still awaited an agreement for compensation before suspending sales.

During August 1998, when the promised light-water reactor had not arrived, North Korea launched a three-state rocket, claiming that a satellite had been launched. Washington then correctly suspected that a missile had been tested, especially when one flew over Japan. Pyongyang also stopped work on the canning project and threatened to go back to the nuclear project. When a false press report suggested that a secret nuclear project was ongoing, Washington demanded an inspection of the site, and Pyongyang refused on the ground that American compensation was still not forthcoming. But when the United States offered food aid, North Korea allowed inspectors, who proved that the press article was wrong.

Round 3 (October 1–2, 1998)

There were no changes in positions. Pyongyang then flatly rejected the American proposal to join the Missile Technology Control Regime, claiming that the United States was violating the Agreed Framework by not lifting sanctions.

When word of the failure of the talks reached Congress, members demanded a review of the relationship. In late 1998, President Bill Clinton defused the situation by appointing a special representative—former Secretary of Defense William Perry, who promised a lifting of some restrictions on banking, trade, and travel and some economic aid (Sigal 2002). In response,

Pyongyang then announced a moratorium on missile tests, which lasted eight years.

Round 4 (March 29–31, 1999)

The United States agreed to consider sanctions relief if North Korea would stop missile development and proliferation activities. Both sides agreed to a fifth round but did not set a date.

Later in 1999, when an American inspection team was admitted to a suspected secret nuclear site, no evidence was found to support rumors about cheating. Perry visited Pyongyang, offering to take concrete steps toward normalization in exchange for North Korean satisfaction of American security concerns by providing a security guarantee. He also promised humanitarian aid as well as a lifting of American sanctions if the DPRK would agree to cease ballistic missile development and proliferation.

Round 5 (September 7–12, 1999)

North Korea agreed to a moratorium on testing long-range missiles. The United States agreed to lift some but not all economic sanctions and did so the following year.

During a meeting in November, the two sides discussed bilateral relations and a high-level North Korean visit to Washington. KEDO finally signed a contract in 2000 to begin construction of two light-water reactors—but six years after the Agreed Framework had been signed!

In 2000, during Clinton's final year in office, American sanctions were imposed on a North Korean firm for proliferating missiles, possibly to Iran, and for receiving centrifuges from Pakistan. Nevertheless, American inspectors were again allowed to visit the suspected nuclear weapons site and found nothing new.

Kim Dae Jung was elected South Korean president in 1998. When he met his North Korean counterpart in 2000, they agreed on several cooperative measures (Lee 2012). In response, Washington relaxed several sanctions, thereby allowing trade, investment and direct personal and commercial financial transactions. North Korea responded by assuring that the moratorium on missile tests would continue.

Round 6 (July 12, 2000)

North Korea monetized the previous request for compensation—$1 billion per year to end exports of missile technology. The United States counteroffered economic normalization if Pyongyang would satisfy all American security concerns.

Later in July, U.S. Secretary of State Madeleine Albright held talks with DPRK Foreign Minister Paek Nam Sun during a forum in Bangkok. However, they did not discuss a proposal, floated ten days earlier by Kim Jong Il in the press, which promised to stop developing rockets if another country would agree to launch its satellites so that North Korea could enter the Internet age.

Round 7 (September 27, 2000)

Talks were held at the UN, but there was no progress on nuclear issues or missiles. However, a joint statement emerged regarding terrorism.

North Korea hoped that Clinton would visit Pyongyang and finally conclude a peace treaty, whereupon the nuclear weapons program would be terminated. During early October, North Korea's second in command visited Washington, delivering a letter to President Clinton. He also met with Albright and Secretary of Defense William Cohen. Pyongyang agreed to freeze deployment, development, exports, production, and testing of missiles over the range of 300 km (186 miles). The United States rejected the offer, wanting the existing facilities and stockpiles also removed. After the Iran Nonproliferation Act was passed that year, new sanctions were slapped on North Korea. Clinton reportedly feared that such a visit to Pyongyang would jeopardize presidential election prospects for Al Gore.

Twelve days later, Albright flew to Pyongyang to meet Kim Jong Il. In their Joint Communique, Kim promised not to test missiles again, and both sides agreed to negotiate a peace treaty that would serve to normalize relations. But she was out of office in four months.

Round 8 (November 1–3, 2000)

No progress occurred. North Korea evidently realized that a Clinton visit to North Korea was not in the cards.

Because of the dispute over the winner of the 2000 election, Clinton announced that he would not travel to North Korea, as someone had to remain in the White House until a new president was declared elected. Eighteen days before he left office, however, sanctions were imposed on a DPRK corporation for violating the Iran Nonproliferation Act of 2000.

Bush Reverses Progress and North Korea Responds

President George W. Bush, who took office in 2001, was cool toward developing a détente with the DPRK (Cha 2002:79). He soon moved the goal posts rather than capitalizing on Albright's achievement. He met with the South Korean president, showing disrespect by not offering to do so with the North along the lines of Albright's breakthrough. He then played tough, demanding that North Korea (still without the promised light-water reactor) must comply with all agreements, stop missile exports, and undertake domestic economic and social reforms. He also slapped more sanctions on the North for shipments to Iran. Although he promised more bilateral talks in 2001, he reversed himself in January 2002: Without citing any specific provocation, he blasted North Korea as part of an Axis of Evil and abandoned the Agreed Framework later that year; his pretext was the belief that North Korea was secretly developing nuclear weapons. Some believe that Pyongyang had cheated during 2001, violating the Agreed Framework (Mathews 2017). But Washington had already cheated on the agreement by holding up the promised light-water reactor since 1994, so if North Korea did in fact return to nuclear power development, Bush's duplicity would have played a role.

Secretary of State Colin Powell was more conciliatory, indicating that Pyongyang was in compliance with the Agreed Framework and moratorium on missile tests; he then offered to participate in negotiations without preconditions (Perlez 2001). However, word in Washington leaked out that Bush contemplated a nuclear strike as one option, whereupon the DPRK returned the same threat. Bush invited North Korea for talks in July but cancelled them when the two Koreas engaged in a naval skirmish. More sanctions were imposed for a shipment of nuclear technology to gain more foreign exchange, but a journalist reported that they were pro forma according to the law and that Bush wanted to meet Kim.

Yet another backslide by Bush was to demand immediate compliance with IAEA safeguard procedures, contrary to the step-by-step process in the

Agreed Framework. North Korea wanted to stick by the agreement until the promised light-water reactor might become functional.

Next, oil shipments were suspended to North Korea in November 2002. One month later, the DPRK responded by expelling IAEA inspectors.

Also in 2002, UN Ambassador John Bolton engaged in a tirade against North Korea, which in turn objected to the hostile tone yet reassured that the missile testing moratorium would continue. Then Assistant Secretary of State James Kelly went to Pyongyang to announce that Washington had unilaterally cancelled the Agreed Framework. Verbal counterblasts were then exchanged.

After Pyongyang hosted a meeting with Japanese Prime Minister Junichirō Koizumi in 2002 (Kaseda 2003:125), Bush suggested new talks (Slevin 2002). Upon receipt of a favorable response, Assistant Secretary of State James Kelly flew to North Korea the following week to offer a "bold initiative" (Samore 2004:11–12): In exchange for North Korean abandonment of nuclear power facilities, Washington was prepared to transfer $95 million to help North Korea build the light-water reactors promised under the recently voided Agreed Framework (BBC 2002). The monetary transfer did indeed take place, but the initiative was not followed up with what Pyongyang most desired—normalization talks.

North Korea then felt free to return to the period before the Agreed Framework. An announcement was made that nuclear weapons were being developed, whereupon fuel oil deliveries stopped. Two nuclear reactors were re-opened, and IAEA inspectors were booted out of the country.

In 2003, Pyongyang admitted that the nuclear program had been restarted (Samore 2004). Hoping thereby to provoke Washington into starting normalization talks, North Korea promised to resolve the nuclear issue (Shenon 2002). But again Washington insisted that denuclearization must come before normalization negotiations.

Bush opposed normalization talks (Litwak and Daly 2016), which have never been held despite urging by China (Choe 2016b). For many years, Washington continued to offer the carrot of economic aid and the stick of economic sanctions to gain cooperation with the North in order to freeze steps leading toward development of nuclear weapons, while refusing to appreciate that North Korea had urgently been seeking normalization first.

In 2003, North Korea again renounced NPT, re-started one of the nuclear reactors, announced the possession of nuclear weapons, and threatened to resume testing of missiles. Next, sanctions were imposed on a North Korean corporation for supplying missile technology to Pakistan. Then Washington rolled out the Proliferation Security Initiative, to which 105 countries eventually subscribed, to interdict any shipment of nuclear weapons around the world.

News of a meeting with the Japanese prime minister hosted by the DPRK later in 2003 prompted Kelly to return to Pyongyang to offer to buy light-water reactors for DPRK if North Korea would abandon nuclear reactors. But after the purchase took effect, normalization talks did not occur. Washington insisted on normalization after a freeze in nuclear weapons development while Pyongyang wanted normalization negotiations without preconditions. China urged the United States to accept the DPRK offer, but the Bush administration held fast to its position.

After North Korean fighter aircraft intercepted a U.S. spy plane over the Sea of Japan that year, China hosted trilateral talks in Beijing with North Korea and the United States, serving as a prelude to the first round of Six-Party Talks.

Pyongyang preferred bilateral negotiations with the United States, primarily to advance the agenda toward normalization. But Washington refused.

Six-Party Talks

At the urging of several major powers, including a three-day suspension of oil shipments from China (Washington Post 2009), the DPRK agreed to Six-Party denuclearization negotiations in 2003 with China, Japan, Russia, South Korea, and the United States. Bilateral negotiations had not been productive, so mediation offered better prospects. From 2003 to 2007, seven rounds were held in Beijing, with several phases in rounds 4, 5, and 6, until they were discontinued during the administration of Barack Obama. Some success was achieved, nevertheless.

First Round (August 27–29, 2003)

During the first round of talks, attended by deputy-level officials, each country stated an initial position. Issues raised were a security guarantee for North Korea; construction of two light-water reactors to replace the graphite-moderated nuclear power plant, as promised in the Agreed Framework; the right to peaceful uses of nuclear power; normalization of diplomatic and trade relations; and the verifiable and irreversible nuclear disarmament of North Korea. After every delegation made a statement, the group agreed to meet again.

Subsequently, Washington announced opposition to a nonaggression pact with North Korea, and refused to hold bilateral negotiations with the Pyongyang government. In turn, the DPRK said that a nuclear test would be held to prove North Korea's capability.

China soon called for a return to the forum. After President Bush expressed openness to providing informal security assurances short of a nonaggression pact or peace treaty, Kim Jong Il signaled that North Korea would to return to talks.

Second Round (February 25–28, 2004)

The United States demanded unilateral concessions on the part of Pyongyang, in particular "complete, verifiable, and irreversible dismantlement" of its nuclear program. Thanks to mediation by China and Russia, North Korea offered to destroy its nuclear weapons program, but would not discontinue its peaceful nuclear activities. Japan, South Korea, and the United States objected to the latter point, a right guaranteed under Article VI of the NPT. A consensus statement merely reiterated a pledge in 1991 for denuclearization of the Korean peninsula. The statement also included a pledge of Peaceful Coexistence of Participating States, which involved an agreement to reconvene in the event of a crisis.

Third Round (June 23–26, 2004)

South Korea and the United States proposed to achieve denuclearization by identifying a set of stages, with verification after each stage. North Korea insisted on compensation in exchange for accepting a freeze.

After verification of stage #1, when the nuclear program would be suspended, fuel oil would go from China, South Korea, and Russia to North Korea. In stage #2, the nuclear program would be dismantled; when verified, the United States would open bilateral talks with Pyongyang on ending all sanctions. North Korea accepted the plan in principle, though insisting on economic compensation. Talks were suspended to determine whether Bush would be re-elected in November. He was.

In February 2005, North Korea, admitting possession of nuclear weapons, refused to attend future Six-Party Talks, evidently annoyed that Condoleezza

Rice said during her confirmation hearing to become Secretary of State that North Korea was an "outpost of tyranny." Pyongyang then cancelled the moratorium on missile tests, threatened to give nuclear weapons to terrorists, and refused to attend the fourth round. Washington then imposed more sanctions on the North.

Next, China summoned Christopher Hill, the American lead negotiator, to Beijing. Hill reaffirmed a commitment never to attack the North and promised to hold bilateral talks with Pyongyang. As a result, Pyongyang agreed to another round.

Fourth Round, Phase 1 (July 26–August 7, 2005)

The United States conceded that North Korea had a right to peaceful uses of atomic energy. The six delegations then adjourned to attend the meeting of the Association of South-East Asian Nations Regional Forum.

Fourth Round, Phase 2 (September 13–19, 2005)

A seeming breakthrough occurred in 2005, known as the Joint Statement: North Korea promised to follow a verifiable step-by-step process of denuclearization, thus serving as a replacement for the Agreed Framework that had been unilaterally abandoned by the United States. In exchange for dismantling its nuclear weapons program, rejoining the NPT, and accepting inspections, Pyongyang asked the United States to conclude a nonaggression treaty, sign a peace treaty, normalize diplomatic relations, resume suspended fuel oil shipments, ship the promised light-water reactor, and respect North Korea's right to develop nuclear power for peaceful purposes. The United States delegates affirmed disinterest in attacking or invading North Korea, pledged to resume fuel oil shipments, supply the light-water reactor, and put a security guarantee in writing while agreeing to work toward normalization. All five countries promised to increase economic cooperation in energy, investment, and trade with North Korea.

Once again, the United States put normalization as the last step in the process. But Washington then added a new demand—improvement in human rights. North Korea wanted the long-promised light-water reactor before efforts to dismantle its nuclear weapons program would begin.

For the first time, bilateral talks were held between Pyongyang and Washington. On the day after the talks, North Korea insisted on prompt shipment of the light-water reactor, but softened the request a few days later. A major agreement seemed around the corner.

Fifth Round, Phase 1 (November 9–11, 2005)

The Joint Statement issued on September 19 was reaffirmed. But new developments occurred, and the talks ended without progress.

Late in 2005, U.S. sanctions were imposed on North Korea for peddling counterfeit American currency and on some trading companies for sending nuclear material to Libya, while freezing deposits in the Banco Delta Asia of Macau. Pyongyang objected to the latter, offering to resume talks only if the assets were un-frozen (BBC 2006). Washington considered the financial issue separate from the nuclear issue, but not Pyongyang. North Korea then conducted multiple missile tests in July and its first nuclear test on October 9, 2006; four more were held later. In response, the UN Security Council authorized trade sanctions, demanding that North Korea refrain from further nuclear or missile testing, abandon its weapons of mass destruction and missile programs, and immediately rejoin the Six-Party Talks. The resolutions authorized stopping North Korean ships at sea to inspect the cargo and remove any proscribed contents, notably weapons shipments. Pyongyang rejected all the demands.

In mid-2006, all preparations for the light-water reactor were terminated, so the Agreed Framework was truly dead. North Korea then conducted seven missile tests. One was a long-range missile, violating a DPRK pledge made in 1999, but no more missile tests were held for the next three years. The UN Security Council then authorized sanctions against the North, which responded by making a "no first use" pledge and promised never to transfer nuclear weapons while denuclearization talks continued. Pyongyang, citing the economic sanctions and American nuclear capability, next conducted its first underground nuclear test in October 2006 and indicated that more tests would be conducted as long as the United States continued to apply sanctions. As a result of the test, Washington indicated that no humanitarian aid could go to the DPRK, and more sanctions were authorized by the Security Council.

China then mediated between North Korea and the United States, and talks resumed (December 18–22) after Pyongyang reiterated the Joint Statement of September 2005 to abandon the nuclear program if further negotiations were successful. But there was no agreement as long as the $25 million remained frozen, a ploy to get the North to shut down its nuclear reactor at Yongbyon.

Fifth Round, Phase 2 (December 18–22, 2006)

The outcome was to reaffirm the September 2005 agreement. But bilateral negotiations to unfreeze North Korea's bank accounts were unsuccessful. The United States, which then claimed that aid to Libya was in support of terrorism, later admitted that funds had been frozen as a bargaining chip to get North Korea to shut down the Yongbyon reactor.

But the Joint Statement fell apart one month later, when Hill revoked his pledge to respect the right of North Korea for the peaceful development of nuclear power, delayed the light-water reactor shipment again, and reiterated the new condition regarding human rights.

During the winter talks recess, bilateral American–North Korean talks took place in Berlin. Washington promised a partial lifting on the bank account freeze, and Pyongyang agreed to freeze the nuclear program in exchange for 500,000 tons of fuel oil annually.

Fifth Round, Phase 3 (February 8–13, 2007)

In a productive meeting, based on a three-stage plan drawn up by China, the six agreed on initial steps to implement the 2005 Joint Statement over the following 60 days in which North Korea would receive 50,000 tons of fuel oil and then shut down and seal the Yongbyon nuclear facilities, allow IAEA inspection, and discuss a list of its nuclear-related activities with the other parties.

Next, North Korea would disable all plutonium facilities, give a complete accounting of all nuclear-related activities, but keep some of the nuclear program ongoing, whereupon another shipment of the same amount of fuel oil would go to the DPRK. Washington would then lift economic sanctions, including removing North Korea from the list of state sponsors of terrorism. In the final stage, discussions would begin to halt missile and nuclear programs and sales as well as US–DPRK normalization talks. For the first time, Pyongyang dropped the requirement that normalization negotiations should precede missile and nuclear disarmament. Five working groups were to design details.

The United States agreed to engage in normalization talks and again pledged to remove North Korea from its list of state sponsors of terrorism, thereby removing the pretext for the bank sanctions. All parties promised to provide emergency shipments of 50,000 tons of heavy fuel oil within 60 days. All six offered to negotiate a permanent peace regime for the peninsula at a separate forum. Five working groups were then organized to design plans to implement the Joint Statement (Lee 2012:167); the groups were to meet within 30 days. When the working groups finished their work, a ministerial-level meeting was to agree to an implementation plan. Meanwhile, North Korea shut down the Yongbyon reactor (Kaku 2012).

Sixth Round, Phase 1 (May 19–22 and July 18–20, 2007)

Although the American negotiator promised that North Korean bank funds were being unfrozen, the money had still not been released due to a Bank of China processing delay, so North Korea negotiators refused to attend until the money was transferred. The other five continued talks, awaiting North Korea's decision to return. Accordingly, a recess was declared.

Russia then decided to handle the bank transfer, fuel aid was shipped from South Korea, and IAEA inspectors declared that Yongbyon had been closed. When talks resumed in July, the parties reaffirmed the Joint Statement of 2005. The working groups were given deadlines for their reports. The first phase of implementation had been completed.

Sixth Round, Phase 2 (September 27–30, 2007)

North Korea again outlined steps toward normalization and a replacement of the armistice agreement with a peace treaty (Kim and Feffer 2008). Washington then removed the DPRK from the list of terrorist states. The working groups submitted their reports, so a second phase implementation plan was agreed upon, calling for three key nuclear facilities at the Yongbyon complex to be disabled and for a complete accounting of all North Korean nuclear activities, both by the end of the year. The DPRK also pledged not to transfer nuclear materials, technology, or know-how to other parties. The other parties agreed to increase aid to North Korea to a total of 1 million tons of heavy fuel oil or fuel oil equivalents and to a continuation of the diplomatic normalization processes. Washington officials offered humanitarian aid on seeing evidence of the disabling of Yongbyon. The Six-Party Talks then ended on the belief that all problems would soon be under control.

During October 2007, when Somali pirates forced their way aboard a North Korean merchant ship, U.S. Navy ships dispatched personnel to overpower the pirates, free the crew, and treat the wounded (Purefoy 2007), winning praise from Pyongyang. The DPRK signed an agreement to denuclearize in exchange for the receipt of humanitarian aid, and more American funds were supplied to the North for fuel aid in exchange for the promise to shut down the Yongbyon nuclear facility (Scanlon 2007). However, when Pyongyang supplied a report of the nuclear inventory in November (before the deadline), the United States objected that the report was incomplete and suspended the promised aid shipment.

But the DPRK insisted that the report was in compliance with phase 2 requirements and slowed down disablement at Yongbyon. In March 2008, the North satisfied the United States by submitting an 18,000-page report, with a cover letter pledging never to export nuclear material again. (An earlier shipment to Syria had been revealed).

Even so, during 2008, North Korea accepted all American demands for inspection—that is, without the precondition of normalization talks on which Pyongyang had once insisted. IAEA inspections then went ahead (Guardian 2008). Progress continued in mid-2008 after Pyongyang made more concessions, providing the United States with extensive details of its nuclear program and efforts to dismantle the Yongbyon facility. The DPRK also renounced terrorist actions, whereupon the Bush administration eased sanctions on the regime and finally removed North Korea from the State Sponsors of Terrorism list. The New York Philharmonic performed in Pyongyang that same year.

But in August, evidently suspicious that the DPRK was developing nuclear capabilities in secret sites, Bush suddenly reversed himself, trying to force Pyongyang into agreeing to a bilateral deal outside the Six-Party agreement: He wanted North Korea to agree to short-notice inspections as a condition of removing DPRK from the list of terrorist states. The other five countries objected. North Korea emphatically rejected the idea. Insisting that inspections be limited to Yongbyon, North Korea responded to the proposal by announcing a reversal of disablement actions and indicated that the reprocessing plant would be restarted. Christopher Hill then went to Pyongyang, and the two parties agreed that short-notice inspections could occur, but only if the DPRK consented. In early October, China, Japan, Russia, South Korea, and the United States then adopted a verbal agreement to ask North Korea to allow inspections outside of Yongbyon. Separately, the two Korean leaders held a summit conference, pledging to work toward a peace treaty.

Seventh Round (December 8–11, 2008)

When the Six-Party Talks resumed, there was no agreement on the final phase of implementation. Pyongyang had completed eight out of eleven dismantlement steps, but plutonium had not yet been de-weaponized. More time was clearly needed for completion of the remaining three steps.

North Korea became frustrated that the latest fuel oil shipment had not arrived, as promised. Progress suddenly came to a halt and was not resumed. Pyongyang failed to agree to a verification protocol for its nuclear program by the end of 2008, when the nuclear program was restarted, and IAEA inspectors were turned away in an effort to pressure American negotiators to live up to the provisions of the Joint Statement.

Obama Years: Cooperation Fizzles

In January 2009, Barack Obama entered the White House, having promised during the 2008 election campaign to resolve issues with several countries by meeting leaders without preconditions. His advisers urged him not to do so. Pyongyang was awaiting fuel oil shipments when he took office, but instead 240,000 tons of food aid (mostly biscuits) were sent. The third phase of implementation could not take place until the fuel oil reached North Korea.

In April 2009, North Korea launched a communications satellite, which was not specifically prohibited by the February 2007 agreement. But Obama saw the launch as a violation, stopped the food aid, and asked the UN Security Council to impose sanctions. China and Russia objected, but Washington insisted on its own sanctions. The DPRK then announced an intention to withdraw from the Six-Party Talks. The situation escalated thereafter.

Obama failed to negotiate with North Korea while in office, preferring a low-key policy of "strategic patience," which meant that he would impose sanctions to tighten pressures, hoping that the economic pain would eventually force Pyongyang to stop nuclear developments. Reference to "all options are on the table" in 2009 and over the years by American decision-makers has been interpreted to imply that the United States had been contemplating a first strike all along (Sagan 2017:75–76).

Obama also asked China to communicate the message to North Korea that nuclear developments must stop. The subtext of the policy was the hope that the DPRK would collapse. That past sanctions had yielded little did not discourage more sanctions so long as China and Russia went along, as they did while he was in office.

But North Korea had established offices in China with Chinese employees as intermediaries, thereby improving their trading capability (Meyers 2015). And North Korea's economy was improving (Hastings 2016). The expectation that sanctions would work was, in short, a mirage. Hardly any country in the world has ever yielded to the pressure of sanctions (Pape 1997).

When the Six-Party Talks did not resume, North Korea proceeded to develop its deterrent. American and IAEA inspectors were told to leave, and the nuclear program went forward with plutonium extraction and another nuclear test, resulting in more sanctions.

Obama then announced continuing support for the Proliferation Security Initiative. South Korea, which in 2008 had elected a hawkish president, signed on. Pyongyang considered Seoul's action to be a violation of the 1953 armistice agreement, the equivalent of a declaration of war.

Statements back and forth between South and North Korea were considered provocations. The two countries were involved in a naval skirmish in 2008 and another in 2009, the latter resulting in more American sanctions.

In 2009, North Korea attempted unsuccessfully to launch a satellite but did launch eight missiles. After UN condemnation, Pyongyang announced withdrawal from the Six-Party Talks. An underground nuclear test later that year also led to increased UN sanctions.

North Korea evidently began to arrest American citizens in 2009 as a ploy to attract attention that might involve diplomacy. Former President Bill Clinton went to Pyongyang that year, and two Americans were released. Washington then proposed talks, and the DPRK agreed. But there were no communications until December, when the State Department sent former diplomat Steven Bosworth to Pyongyang, yielding ambiguous results.

Former President Jimmy Carter arranged for the release of another American in 2010 (Kim and Smith 2017). Carter then reported that North Korea was willing to resume the Six-Party Talks without preconditions to achieve denuclearization. Washington demanded that the DPRK must abandon the nuclear program before any talks would occur—in effect, refusing to return to the February 2007 implementation agreement and thus moving the goal posts again.

In July and October 2011, Washington and Pyongyang held bilateral discussions. North Korea was willing to return to the Six-Party Talks without preconditions. After another naval skirmish between the two Koreas occurred, China urged resumption of the Six-Party Talks. Japan, South Korea, and the United States turned down the invitation. In November 2010, when North Korea offered to give up "thousands" of fuel rods as a conciliatory gesture, Washington did not respond to the offer. Instead, American negotiators demanded that the North demonstrate its commitment to abandon its nuclear program prior to resuming talks as if there had been no implementation process in the February 2007 agreement.

After Kim Jong Il's death in December 2011, his son Kim Jong Un took the helm. In domestic affairs, he opened the economy to allow merchants to keep their profits. In international matters, he announced a freeze on nuclear weapons, a halt to long-range missile tests, suspension of uranium enrichment, and he invited back nuclear inspectors. China then hosted bilateral talks, resulting in an agreement on Leap Year Day 2012, in which the United States offered food aid and 240,000 tons of fuel oil in return for a North Korea moratorium on uranium enrichment, and missile and nuclear testing as well as a return of IAEA inspectors, whereupon Six-Party Talks would resume. But DPRK missiles were launched later during 2012, so the Leap Year Day Agreement was in jeopardy.

Because North Korea's launch of a satellite seemingly contradicted the pledge, the third UN authorization of sanctions followed, and the fourth in 2013 due to another nuclear weapons test. American food aid stopped as a result. North Korea conducted another nuclear weapons test in 2013, and an American spy plane flew over North Korea.

The DPRK tried to attract attention in March 2013 by announcing that the previously pledged nonaggression pact with South Korea was void, the border between the two countries was closed, and the direct telephone line between the two governments was shut down. In response, for the first time, American B-2 stealth bombers flew over South Korea and possibly elsewhere on the peninsula (Shanker and Choe 2013); others were planned, aimed at reassuring Seoul (Choe 2013b). Pyongyang then threatened to attack the United States, testing six short-range missiles while putting rockets on standby alert (MacAskill 2013).

Nevertheless, the DPRK called for a peace treaty in May to replace the armistice. Throughout the year, North Korea made several more proposals (cf. Choe 2013a), stating that the Military Armistice Commission and Neutral Nations Supervisory Commission were supposed to be temporary bodies and therefore should be replaced by a peace treaty. But Washington was still committed to await unmistakable DPRK moves to denuclearize before talks on normalization or a peace treaty could begin, a policy contained in a letter written by Obama to Kim Jong Un delivered by State Department official Stephen Bosworth in 2013. North Korea also implied that removal of American troops from the South is a precondition for denuclearization, a demand that Washington has consistently rejected.

In September 2013, Beijing tried to renew the Six-Party process, despite a report that the North had restarted its Yongbyon facility. The Chinese government held an unusual commemorative ceremony marking the tenth anniversary of the launch of the Six-Party Talks, but American, Japanese, and South Korean representatives boycotted, lacking North Korean commitments. At the meeting, North Korea's First Vice Minister called again for the resumption of dialogue "without preconditions."

American citizens were arrested in 2013, 2014, and 2016 (Perlez 2013; CNN 2014; Reuters 2016), an evident ploy to have Washington dispatch negotiators to secure their release while repeating the desire for negotiations for normalization without preconditions. A Hollywood film disrespectfully portraying Kim Jong Un in 2014 led to a cyberattack on the studio producing the film. DPRK cyberattack capabilities are among the strongest in the world, and more are anticipated. Meanwhile, Washington sought to cyberhobble Pyongyang's nuclear development program (Sanger and Broad 2017).

Three American hostages were released during 2014. Negotiations were handled by James Clapper, Director of National Intelligence. Former UN Ambassador Bill Richardson played a role in gaining the release of one of the three.

On March 25, 2014, hours after the United States, South Korea and Japan held an extraordinary three-way summit meeting to discuss the DPRK nuclear buildup, North Korea fired more rockets and launched more missiles and then exchanged hundreds of artillery shells across the disputed sea border with South Korea. More missile tests were held almost monthly. After the UN Commission on Human Rights referred North Korean human rights violations to the International Criminal Court, Pyongyang threatened to conduct another nuclear test on the same day that a DPRK envoy in Moscow indicated willingness to resume the Six-Party Talks. During most of the year, the United States made assessments of North Korea's military capabilities, and then in early 2015 imposed more sanctions.

After offering to suspend nuclear testing if South Korea and the United States would call off annual joint military exercises, North Korea conducted more missile tests on five separate occasions during 2015, resulting in more sanctions. No American diplomacy was undertaken to stop the downward trend.

The last straw apparently for the North came sometime in 2016. In January, diplomats of both countries discussed resumption of talks, but Washington demurred when the DPRK representative insisted on negotiations toward a peace treaty with Seoul and Washington. During March, the South Korean–United States military exercises, which Seoul characterized as "the largest ever," included an American nuclear submarine for the first time since 1991. The exercises involved a maneuver to train troops how to conquer Pyongyang and kill top leaders. Then in July, Obama designated Kim Jong Un as a human rights abuser; he was added to the embargo list, implementing the North Korea Sanctions and Policy Enhancement Act passed in February.

In response, North Korea threatened nuclear war, launched missiles, and set off a nuclear bomb. Yet Pyongyang was still asking for a peace treaty before denuclearization (AP 2016a), while Washington continued to maintain that negotiations for such a peace treaty would occur only after North Korea took "irreversible steps toward denuclearization"; although Pyongyang responded by agreeing to talk on that basis, Washington did not listen (Carlin 2016).

Pyongyang arrested yet another American that year and conducted a test of a hydrogen bomb, the latter prompting the United States to speed up equipping South Korea with an anti-missile system. When China objected, the American response was to ask Beijing to prevail on North Korea to stop developing its deterrent.

Washington interpreted North Korea's testing as a violation of UN resolutions, and the UN Security Council imposed more sanctions. Washington then threatened to extend secondary sanctions, which would mean that any company doing business with North Korea would be embargoed (Choe 2016b). Although secondary sanctions reportedly got Iran to the bargaining table, those involving the DPRK were primarily aimed at China. But Beijing failed to put firm pressure on North Korea, evidently fearing that the regime might collapse, resulting in unification of the peninsula by South Korea. Since China did not quickly apply them, and shipments went unchallenged during nighttime, North Korean officials claimed that the sanctions did not bother them (Perlez and Huang 2016; Fifield 2016; AP 2016a). Some estimates then appeared that by 2020 North Korea would have at least 20 nuclear warheads mounted on ballistic missiles (Litwak and Daly 2016).

In mid-2016, Pyongyang launched a long-range missile, claiming that the objective was to put a satellite into orbit. Washington interpreted the move as an indication that the DPRK had the technology to hit the continental United States, consistent with verbal threats that year. The American response was to proceed with plans, delayed from an announcement to do so in 2009, to deploy an anti-missile defense system of uncertain capability in South Korea (Choe 2016a). China then objected, promising economic retaliation against Seoul and accusing the United States of altering the strategic regional balance (Makinen and Borowiec 2016). Washington, in turn, urged Beijing to prevail on North Korea to stop the arms race. But China then urged the United States to get back to the bargaining table with the North.

At the end of July 2016, North Korea announced that the only means of contact—at the UN in New York—would be cut off because the United States put the leader, Kim Jong Un, on a list to be subjected to sanctions for violating human rights, implementing the North Korea Sanctions and Policy Enhancement Act passed in February. Pyongyang interpreted the action as tantamount to a declaration of war (AP 2016b).

Anti-personnel mines were installed by the North along the DMZ in August, whereupon the UN Command protested that the armistice agreement bans armed guards and weapons within the DMZ (KBS 2016). On September 8, North Korea conducted its fifth and most powerful nuclear test. In all, North Korea during the year 2016 conducted two nuclear and twenty-four missile tests (Delury 2017:48).

In the final days of the presidency of Barack Obama, China criticized the United States for not negotiating on a regular basis, and the United States responded that North Korea refused to denuclearize (Choe 2016b). Washington claimed to be tired of North Korean offers to make concessions followed by repeatedly reneging on promises (Litwak and Daly 2016), though the same could be said about the United States over the years. Negotiations were off the table in Washington because none of the actions from Pyongyang to develop a nuclear deterrent were interpreted as invitations for talks.

Escalation and De-Escalation under Trump

Campaigning for president, Donald Trump promised to meet Kim Jong Un once elected. Back-channel talks were indeed scheduled by Trump but were cancelled after the apparent assassination of Kim's half-brother (Demick 2017). Once again, an American president proved untrustworthy.

Then in mid-March 2017, Secretary of State Rex Tillerson declared an end to the policy of "strategic patience" (Gearan and Fifield 2017). The new policy at first appeared to be a military option, as he indicated that the United States would attack North Korea when an unspecified "red line" was crossed. Soon afterward, North Korea tested a revved-up rocket engine. When more missile testing occurred, American warships were dispatched to the Sea of Japan along with various hostile comments. Nevertheless, missile tests defiantly continued, and the U.S. Air Force launched a missile into the Pacific in response (Choe 2017; Rocha 2017).

During May, a cyberattack hit targets in the United States and such allies as Britain and South Korea (Riley and Mullen 2017), the largest such effort since the retaliation against Sony Pictures in 2014. The aim of the attack was to demand money in Bitcoins before anyone's computer would be allowed to function again, presumably to secure relief from economic sanctions.

To attract American negotiators, the DPRK tried again to arrest Americans. An American diplomat, the State Department specialist on North Korea, was dispatched from Washington to gain the release of one, coinciding with a visit by basketball star Dennis Rodman to Pyongyang. Soon, the existence of a back-channel for over a year, with a high-level Korean negotiator, was revealed (Solomon 2017). One American, arrested in 2016, was released in a coma during June, but three Americans were still held as hostages (Kim and Smith 2017). Otherwise, there were no open negotiations during 2017.

Instead, the sanctions option was explored (cf. Stanton, Lee, Klingner 2017). Trump counted on China to carry them out to restrain North Korea, but Beijing was hesitant. When the United States sought more sanctions to be authorized by the UN Security Council at one point, Russia vetoed the proposal but later approved. Congress then adopted a sanctions bill (which also included Iran and Russia), and Trump signed the law, albeit opposed to those involving Moscow.

DPRK missile tests continued (Hennigan 2017), including an apparent intercontinental ballistic missile, followed by a similar American missile test (Sullivan and Cooper 2017). DPRK tests, fourteen through the end of July 2017 included four long-range tests, two over Japanese territory. Tests led to denunciations by the United States and more sanctions. North Korea responded with yet another acerbic comment. Much tougher Security Council sanctions, aimed at cutting Pyongyang's $3 billion export market by one-third (Harris 2017; Kaiman 2017), were then unanimously approved by the Security Council. Washington went ahead with secondary sanctions, naming six Chinese firms, two from Singapore, and one in Russia (Morello 2017).

When North Korea continued testing and threatening in midsummer 2017, President Trump all of a sudden threatened that the United States was ready to attack, using rhetoric that matched the colorful language of Pyongyang. Earlier, Trump insisted that North Korea would never be allowed to have nuclear weapons. Now, Trump indicated that North Korea's possession of a nuclear warhead crossed a red line. But both "red lines" were crossed with impunity.

Although tentative plans for an American preventive war were revealed by Defense Secretary James "Mad Dog" Mattis, the verbal volley from Trump prompted Mattis, Secretary of State Tillerson, and Joint Chiefs of Staff General Joseph Dunford to assure the world that Washington had no intention of going any farther toward the brink of war (McManus 2017). Tillerson assured Pyongyang that the United States did not seek regime change and indicated that negotiations were the preferred option, but only after an end to repeated testing (ibidem).

North Korea, which has long favored negotiations, indicated that its nuclear capability would never be bargained away and also that both Japan and South Korea need not fear nuclear attacks—just the United States. Tillerson appeared to be whistling in the wind about negotiations, as the budget of the understaffed Department of State was slated for major cuts, doubtless depriving him of the infrastructure for serious diplomacy.

The DPRK continued with harsh rhetoric as usual, but suddenly Trump responded that the United States would respond to another "threat" as a red line for a military response (Hennigen, Cloud, Bierman 2017). Pyongyang then called that bluff by threatening to send missiles near Guam, whereupon Trump upped the ante with an even more bellicose statement. Despite mixed signals from Washington, North Korea did not put troops on alert and soon backed down from threatening to attack Guam.

Beijing, meanwhile, criticized both North Korea and the United States for their harsh rhetoric. During July, China and Russia reported that North Korea would consider freezing the current nuclear program if the United States would freeze military exercises with South Korea, whereupon negotiations could begin (Buncombe 2017). But Washington refused, insisting on a nuclear freeze before talks.

When Chinese military exercises impressed Graham Allison (2017) as a hint that an American army sent to conquer North Korea would face Chinese defenders with greater military capabilities (cf. Micklethwaite 2017), Beijing quickly announced a policy of neutrality if war broke out between the United States and the DPRK yet agreed to enforce sanctions—that is, unless they were imposed on Chinese firms (Denyer 2017).

But if negotiations at high levels were to be held to defuse the war of words, the problem was that North Korea said that denuclearization would never be on the agenda. And no United States leaders were prepared to tolerate a nuclear-armed DPRK. Washington's only option, however remote, was to pray that sanctions would force Pyongyang to reconsider. For a time, the verbal volleys stopped, though Trump twice indicated opposition to diplomacy (Landler 2017) despite assurances from Tillerson that diplomacy was ongoing and would move to a higher level if weapons tests stopped.

The tension level then subsided until yet another set of military exercises by South Korea and the United States. When asked why they were being conducted in the precarious atmosphere, a Defense Department statement claimed that they were "defensive" (Kim 2017). But they were "war games," involving a demolition of North Korea, including the assassination of Kim Jong Un, clearly an offensive exercise. As usual, war games were met with a hostile response from North Korea—more missile tests and a nuclear explosion from the North which purported to be a hydrogen bomb that could fit into an intercontinental ballistic missile.

In response, Defense Secretary Mattis indicated that a threat to use force would result in a "massive military response" (Nussbaum, Bender, Griffiths 2017). Yet Pyongyang had regularly made threats, demonstrating colorblindness toward "red lines" and no reluctance to stop the same kinds of war threats.

One part of the war games involved South Korea testing a missile of its own. Subsequently, efforts began to revise the mutual defense treaty with the United States to allow Seoul to develop ballistic missiles with a range of up to 500 miles and a payload weight of up to 1,100 pounds (Smith-Spark, Lee, Treyz 2017). Meanwhile, Trump threatened to cut off all trade with any country that did business with North Korea. Effective September 1, the United States passport would no longer be valid for anyone in North Korea, stranding about 200 American humanitarian workers (Dias 2017).

Perhaps the most fascinating commentary on American diplomacy regarding North Korea occurred on September 6 and 7, when Russia hosted talks in Vladivostok with Japan and South Korea (three-party talks). The United

States was not invited. While Washington was trying to increase economic sanctions, Moscow was evidently prepared to make up any DPRK economic shortfalls and reported that the DPRK nuclear program would be frozen if the United States offered negotiations without preconditions (Baron 2017). One week later, after Trump denounced the idea of negotiations with the DPRK, the latter not only threatened to reduce the United States to "ashes and darkness" but also rescinded the pledge never to attack Japan (Kim and Takenaka 2017). North Korea then conducted its fourteenth missile test of the year, two of which were ICBMs (McLaughlin and Martinez 2017).

Then came Trump's address to the United Nations, in which he threatened devastating war with North Korea and insulted Kim Jong Un as "Little Rocket Man" in front of the world. The DPRK foreign minister then responded with a counter-insult—that Trump was "deranged"—but also claimed that an attack on the continental United States was "inevitable" (Demick and Hennigan 2017). In his speech Trump further encouraged members of the UN to pursue their own self-interest, evidently not realizing that he had provided a justification for North Korea to pursue a deterrent force.

Later, Trump indicated that Kim would "not be around much longer," which the foreign minister interpreted as an "act of war," giving North Korean artillery the right to shoot down American airplanes near but outside its airspace. The tit-for-tat, thus, reached a level where war did seem inevitable.

Nevertheless, Secretary of State Rex Tillerson indicated that negotiations would be sought. He promised that if missile tests stopped for sixty days, then talks could begin.

Instead, the United States persuaded members of the UN Security Council to impose tighter sanctions in September. North Korea considered the September sanctions an act of "genocide," because of the effect on ordinary people (Blanchard and Shim 2017).

During October, a Russian report indicated that North Korea would consider freezing the current nuclear program if normalization and peace talks began with the United States (PressTV 2017), something that Washington had consistently refused, insisting on the freeze before talks. Later that month, after a South Korean fishing vessel intruded into North Korean waters, the crew and ship were seized at first but later released, giving yet another sign of not wanting to provoke retaliation (NYT 2017).

During a ten-day trip to four Asian countries, President Donald Trump continued to demand denuclearization of North Korea prior to negotiations. After talks in Beijing, China agreed to send a high-level envoy to Pyongyang.

However, rather than carrying Trump's message, the proposal was for a freeze in American war games in exchange for a freeze in missile and nuclear tests (Lockie 2017). The Chinese proposal, the same advocated for years, was accepted by North Korea, but rejected by the United State.

By mid-November, a brand new set of war games was held involving three aircraft carriers with F/A-18 fighter jets and B-1 bombers along with naval vessels from Japan and South Korea (Lendon 2017). In addition, F-35 stealth fighter jets were deployed to an American base in Okinawa for the first time. The show of force clearly gave the impression that they were poised for an immediate attack, though Trump said that he hoped that they would not be used. When Russia objected that the exercises were too provocative, the United States response was that they would be more discrete, but the exercises continued, and Pyongyang objected that they signaled that war was inevitable (PressTV 2017).

And, just before Thanksgiving, the president put North Korea on the list of state sponsors of terrorism, upping the level of sanctions thereby. The apparent pretext was the assassination of Kim Jong Un's half-brother and apparent torture of an American held prisoner in the DPRK who died shortly after his release (Nakamura 2017).

On November 28, North Korea launched its third ICBM in the middle of the night, declaring "with pride" that the country had become a "rocket power" (Morello and Denyer 2017). Although detected by the United States, the missile was not shot down. In response, President Trump not only condemned the launch, called Kim "a sick puppy," begged China to increase pressure, and ordered an uptick in sanctions. The American ambassador to the United Nations asked all countries to sever commercial and diplomatic ties with the DPRK and for Beijing to cut off all oil supplied to North Korea. Subsequently, more than twenty countries have either downgraded relations or expelled DPRK diplomats, but the oil still flows.

Nevertheless, instead of agreeing to a ninth round of sanctions, Russia's UN ambassador responded by urging Pyongyang to stop all testing and for the United States to cancel military drills scheduled for December in order to stop the continuing "spiral of tension" (ibidem). China, in turn, scolded the United States for raising tensions and missing opportunities for negotiation since Trump took office. Beijing also asked both sides to lower the inflammatory rhetoric (PressTV 2017).

During late 2017, an emissary from the United Nations went to Pyongyang. Although he sought to cool down the situation, he failed. Jeffrey

Feltman, UN Under-Secretary-General for Political Affairs, undertaking the first official UN visit to North Korea in six years, met Ri Yong Ho, North Korean Foreign Minister. Although they agreed that the situation was "dangerous," Feltman reported that Kim would not seriously negotiate until North Korea had attained a position of strength at the bargaining table, so he would continue to test weapons in violation of UN Security Council sanctions (Krever and Berliner 2017). Feltman stressed the need for diplomacy before miscalculation would lead to war.

In early December, Dennis Rodman offered to lead a diplomatic mission to Pyongyang. He also proposed a confidence-building measure—a basketball game involving Guam and North Korea (Pentchoukov 2017). However, the United States had long given up providing measures to develop mutual trust.

Then on December 12, 2017, Secretary of State Rex Tillerson announced that the United States was ready to negotiate with Pyongyang "without preconditions." He qualified his statement as urging North Korea to come to the table with the idea of changing the situation. Afterward, the White House reiterated that denuclearization steps would have to precede negotiations (Spetalnick and Brunnstrom 2017). And Tillerson soon reversed himself, returning to the view that denuclearization must come before negotiations (Morello 2017). There could be no clearer signal to Pyongyang that leaders of the United States remained untrustworthy, thereby serving as a pretext to justify continuing nuclear weapons development.

More UN Security Council sanctions were voted in December (Lederer 2017). Crude oil shipments to North Korea were to be limited to 4 million barrels annually—10 percent of the country's current intake (Blanchard and Shim 2017), considered as an "act of war" by the DPRK. Another measure, asking countries to recall North Koreans working abroad, was to be completed by the end of 2019. Yet the same resolution called for resumption of the Six-Party Talks.

When 2018 began, both Kim and Trump exchanged more negative messages. But in early January 2018, the DPRK called for talks with the ROK, something that the newly elected South Korean President Moon Jae In had been requesting since his election earlier in 2017. The Winter Olympic Games were scheduled to be held in South Korea during February 2018, and Moon offered to discuss the matter with the North (Grohmann 2017). The complication was that the United States planned to hold war games in January, so Moon asked for their postponement. But Washington did not immediately respond. Instead, the White House at first viewed the DPRK initiative as an effort to split Seoul from Washington (Denyer 2018), not realizing that South Koreans might be tired of the American strategy of continually pitting the North against the South and thereby maintaining a constant atmosphere of crisis with a valuable ally. Nevertheless, Washington eventually decided to postpone war games until after the Olympics. North Korea then formally accepted Moon's offer for negotiations at Panmunjom, where the two Koreas agreed that North Korean athletes could participate in the Winter Olympics, including joint appearances. In addition, Pyongyang was allowed to send its symphony orchestra and other performers to Seoul and the Olympics (Fifield 2018a). Trump, after flattering himself into believing that his pressure produced negotiations that he had formerly opposed, then indicated that he was open to a telephone conversation with Kim after various unspecified preconditions were met (Oliphant 2018). Moon, clearly aware that flattery works wonders with Trump, congratulated Trump for bringing about the talks due to American military pressure (Boyer 2018), while Russia's Vladimir Putin believed that Kim outwitted Trump (Rajaman 2018). However, Moon's positive remark about Trump provoked Pyongyang to threaten a boycott (Stiles 2018b). ROK diplomats then presumably informed their DPRK counterparts that they were only trying to calm the unpredictable White House occupant.

In early January 2018, Trump was quoted as saying that the United States was not considering a preemptive strike and would instead rely on "peace through strength" (Borger and McCurry 2018). But at the end of the month, while the idea of a limited American strike to give North Korea a "bloody nose" was still being considered, the first nominee for ambassador to South Korea was withdrawn because he strongly opposed such a provocation, evidently expecting that Pyongyang would retaliate (Fifield 2018b).

After South Korean President Moon met Kim in February 2018, the situation improved. Expressing the desire to meet Trump, Kim said that he was willing to undertake "denuclearization," he would allow war games to continue, missile tests would stop, and a nuclear test site would be closed. After Trump accepted Kim's invitation in March, Kim hosted Michael Pompeo in April and May, and released three imprisoned Americans in his second visit.

Trump referred to Kim as "honorable," exchanged words with him on Twitter for 75 minutes, talked with Kim by telephone (Wagner 2018), considered reducing American troops in South Korea, and stated that he opposed regime change. War games were toned down in March and April. And a summit was initially planned for May but later scheduled for June 12. Secretary of State Pompeo promised eventual economic rewards.

Because of the de-escalation, China began to relax sanctions imposed on North Korea. South Korea was making similar plans to restore former economic ties.

On April 29, National Security Adviser John Bolton insisted that denuclearization similar to what happened in Libya (involving the eventual death of the Libyan leader) must precede aid. In mid-May, a new set of war games involved a simulated attack on North Korea, and Pyongyang spotted nuclear-capable B-52 bombers and stealth F-22 fighter jets.

Pyongyang asked for the war games to stop, canceled talks with South Korea, rejected Bolton's scenario, insisted that denuclearization would occur only after America's hostile policy and nuclear threats ended, refused to be blackmailed by economic promises, and thereby cast doubt on the summit (Noack 2018).

Trump's response was equivocal, but Vice President Michael Pence reiterated the relevance of the Libyan Model, whereupon North Korean media attacked him as a "dummy" and said the country was prepared for nuclear war. Trump canceled the summit, citing hostile rhetoric, demanded denuclearization, but kept the door open for a later summit—as did Kim (Choe 2018). The following day, after a conciliatory response from Pyongyang, Trump indicated that he wanted the talks to occur, and positive signals from Pyongyang assured that the June 12 summit would be held in Singapore.

Singapore Declaration

From the first handshake, the summit began on a positive note, as the two leaders established a warm friendship and mutual trust. There was insufficient time to agree to a comprehensive declaration, but the two agreed on measures that two countries had long sought: (1) diplomatic normalization, (2) peace regime, including a treaty to finally end the Korean War, (3) denuclearization of the Korean peninsula, and (4) return of bodies of American soldiers missing in action.

During and after the talks, there was discussion on several more issues – abduction of Koreans from Japan to North Korea, destruction of testing sites, end of war games, human rights, safety for Christians, sanctions relief, and verification procedures (Nakamura et al. 2018). Kim also agreed to shut down a missile launching site after the meeting, a gesture building more confidence, in apparent exchange for Trump's pledge to stop the war games. Further talks have the task of designing step-by-step implementation.

Conclusion

Negotiations between North Korea and the United States proceeded down a much bumpier road than in the case with Hanoi and Washington. Somewhere along the highway, there was a red light signal that would not turn to green. To determine who was primarily responsible, as both sides share blame, there is a need to examine the history of unilateral reciprocated confidence-building measures and negative moves, using a list that leaves out redundant interactive rhetorical threat-and-response elements (Tables 4.1–4.2). The list, compiled with the year as the unit of analysis, does not count all war game components by the United States, which exceed the total number of missile launches and nuclear tests conducted by North Korea. The war games occurred over several days and involved a large number of military units, so statistical equivalence is difficult to determine.

Although the United States seemed obsessed with cheating by North Korea, on several occasions, no such behavior was found when inspections occurred. Pyongyang maintained moratoria on testing for years, while patiently waiting for a promised light-water reactor for nearly a decade. Out of repeated frustration, both sides revoked promises.

The charts reveal that there have been far more confidence-building offers by North Korea than by the United States (Tables 4.1–4.2). Washington's attempt to build confidence most often consisted of relaxing previous onerous burdens placed on North Korea. The Democratic People's Republic of Korea, more vulnerable than the superpower United States, has repeatedly demonstrated more willingness to negotiate and respond positively whenever irritations have been mitigated.

Future prospects for improved relations between North Korea and the United States, however, are much brighter today. Although Pyongyang sought normalization more urgently than the United States, DPRK's technique of making threats to get to the bargaining table may have worked in the past, but such moves later reduced trust in Washington. The bargaining table gathered dust for a decade while the DPRK demonstrated offensive capabilities to the world, and the United States responded in kind.

North Korea has evidently achieved a nuclear deterrent, however modest. The aim, from the deterrence playbook, was to reach a position of nuclear equality, whence normalization could be negotiated from a position of strength. In late November 2017, Pyongyang announced that stage had been reached (Blanchard and Shim 2017).

Mediation seemed appropriate in the past, when North Korea and the United States were angry with each other yet had a common interest in preventing war. China, however, failed. Three Americans (Jimmy Carter, Dennis Rodman, and Bill Richardson) offered their services in 2017 but were ignored. South Korean President Moon Jae In was more successful, though he only relayed messages.

A series of unilateral reciprocated confidence-building measures on the part of North Korea and the United States then assured Kim and Trump that serious negotiations would take place if they met. The first such measure was the American decision to postpone the war games from February to March.

Direct communication was next. Trump could easily explain that his "Rocket Man" comment was a form of praise. Kim would have apologized for his underlings who used unflattering comments about Trump as well as the mistreatment of Otto Warmbier, who died shortly after his release from captivity. Despite those who see leaders as purely ego-driven, there is nothing more important than establishing bonds of friendship in foreign relations. Indeed, they indicated in the text of the later Singapore Declaration that "mutual confidence building" was the precondition for the summit meeting.

Confidence was built as the two leaders reciprocated unilaterally in several measures: Kim froze weapons tests, destroyed a nuclear test site, released three Americans, and reaffirmed commitment to total denuclearization. Trump considered a reduction in military forces in South Korea, promised no regime change, and toned down winter wargames.

More of the same occurred during and after the summit. In all, eleven issues were identified as needing attention. Donald Trump indicated that war games would be stopped in apparent exchange for Kim's promise to destroy a missile test site.

The Singapore Declaration, thus, set the future agenda, identifying goals that cannot quickly be accomplished. Although three scholars have suggested a step-by-step plan for denuclearization (Hecker, Carlin, Serbin 2018), a more comprehensive "road map" is needed to include normalization of relations, a peace treaty, and many other issues. The appropriate model is the "road map" used in achieving normalization of relations between the United States and Vietnam.

Whether such a plan can be devised and carried out became the main challenge after the summit. Lead negotiators on both sides will be directly answerable to the two leaders. Creative diplomacy is needed.

Negotiations promise to be difficult and lengthy, yet positive results may ensue. After all, success was achieved despite almost intractable issues in the case of Vietnam. The prospect of war involving the Korean peninsula has haunted the world for far too long.

References

Allison, Graham (2017). "China's Ready for War," *Los Angeles Times*, August 8.
Associated Press (2016a). "K-Pop and Tensions in the DMZ," *Los Angeles Times*, February 14.
Associated Press (2016b). "North Korea: U.S. Sanctions Against Kim Jong Un Cross 'Red Line'," *nbcnews.com*, July 28. Accessed August 11, 2017.
Bailey, Stephen K. (1992). *The Korean Armistice*. New York: St. Martin's Press.
Baron, Jeff (2017). "What If Sanctions Brought North Korea to the Brink? 'Well, in 1914 …,'" *38north.org*, September 7.
Blanchard, Ben, and Hyonhee Shim (2017). "North Korea Rejects New UN Sanctions, Calls Them an 'Act of War'," *reuters.com*, December 24.
Borger, Julian, and Justin McCurry (2018). "North Korea: Trump Promises 'Peace Through Strength' and Denies Strike Plan," *theguardian.com*, January 10.
Bowring, Philip (1994). "After Kim Il Sung Comes the Reunification Process," *International Herald Tribune*, July 11: 6.
Boyer, Dave (2018). "South Korea's President Credits Trump for Talks with North Korea," *Washington Times*, January 10.
British Broadcasting Corporation (2002). "US Grants N Korea Nuclear Funds," *bbc.com/news*, April 3.
British Broadcasting Corporation (2006). "N. Korea Offers Nuclear Talks Deal," *bbc.com/news*, April 13.
British Broadcasting Corporation (2009). "The End of the Korean War: Does It Matter?," *bbc.com/news*, June 5.
British Broadcasting Corporation (2013). "North Korea Ends Peace Pacts with South," *bbc.com/news*, March 8.
Cable News Network (2014). "Americans Detained in North Korea Speak to CNN, Ask for U.S. Help," *cnn.com*, September 12.
Cable News Network (2017). "Korean War Fast Facts," *cnn.com*, August 2.
Carlin, Robert (2016). "North Korea Said It's Willing to Talk Denuclearization (But No One Noticed)," *thediplomat.com*, July 13. Accessed December 16, 2017.
Cha, Victor (2002). "Korea's Place in the Axis," *Foreign Affairs*, 81 (3): 79–92.

Chen, Jean (2003). *Limits of the "Lips and Teeth" Alliance: An Historical Review of Chinese–North Korea Relations*. Princeton, NJ: Woodrow Wilson Center for Scholars, Asia Program Special Report 115.

Choe Sang-Hun (2013a). "North Korea Sets Conditions for Return to Talks," *New York Times*, April 18.

Choe Sang-Hun (2013b). "North Korea Threatens U.S. Military Bases in the Pacific," *New York Times*, March 21.

Choe Sang-Hun (2016a). "South Korea and U.S. Agree to Deploy Missile Defense System," *New York Times*, July 7.

Choe Sang-Hun (2016b). "U.S. Weighs Tighter Sanctions on North Korea If China Fails to Act," *New York Times*, January 21.

Choe Sang-Hun (2017). "South Korea's Leader Bluntly Warns U.S. Against Striking North," *New York Times*, August 16.

Choe Sang-Hun (2018). "North Korea Willing to Talk About 'Complete Denuclearization'," *New York Times*, May 27.

Collins, Robert (2014). "A Brief History of the US–ROK Combined Military Exercises," 38north.org. Accessed August 3, 2017.

Columbia Broadcasting System (2000). "How Many Americans Died in Korea?," *cbsnews.com*, June 5. Accessed August 3, 2017.

Columbia Broadcasting System (2017a). "A Timeline of North Korea's Nuclear Tests," *cbsnews.com*, September 3. Accessed December 16, 2017.

Columbia Broadcasting System (2017b). "North Korea Missile Tests—A Timeline," *cbsnews.com*, September 6. Accessed November 9, 2017.

Cummings, Bruce (2005). *Korea's Place in the Sun: A Modern History*. New York: Norton.

Demick, Barbara (2017). "Can U.S. and North Korea Get Back to Negotiations?," *Los Angeles Times*, August 11.

Demick, Barbara, and W.J. Hennigan (2017). "North Korea Foreign Minister Says Trump's Insults Make Rocket Attack on U.S. 'Inevitable All the More'," *Los Angeles Times*, September 23.

Denyer, Simon (2017). "China Demands U.S. Immediately Withdraw N. Korea Sanctions, Warns They Will Damage Ties," *Washington Post*, August 24.

Denyer, Simon (2018). "South Korea Welcomes North's Offer of Talks," *Washington Post*, January 2.

Dias, Elizabeth (2017). "The 200 Americans Living in North Korea Have Little Time Left to Leave," *Time*, August 24.

Eckert, Paul (2012). "U.S. Suspends Food Aid to North Korea over Missile Plan," *reuters.com*, March 29.

Far Eastern Economic Review (1989). "Discounting the Debt," *Far Eastern Economic Review*, May 11: 8.

Farrell, John F. (2009). "Team Spirit: A Case Study on the Value of Military Exercises as a Show of Force in the Aftermath of Combat Operations," *Air and Space Power Journal*, 23 (3): 94–100.

Fifield, Anna (2016). "The Voyages of Dawnlight: Where Is It Headed? And What Is It Carrying?," *Washington Post*, February 19.
Fifield, Anna (2017). "Kim Jong Il Calls Trump a 'Mentally Deranged Dotard'," *Washington Post*, September 21.
Fifield, Anna (2018a). "North Korea Says It Will Send a 140-Member Orchestra to Perform in South Korea," *Washington Post*, January 15.
Fifield, Anna (2018b). "Withdrawal of U.S. Envoy Candidate and Tough Talk from Trump Worry South Korea," *Washington Post*, February 1.
Fisher, Max (2016). "North Korea, Far from Crazy, Is All Too Rational," *New York Times*, September 10.
Friedman, Herbert A. (2013). "The Cold War in Korea—Operation Jilli." *www.psywarrior.com/OpnJilli.html*. Accessed January 16, 2018.
Gearan, Anne, and Anna Fifield (2017). "Tillerson Says 'All Options Are on the Table' When It Comes to North Korea," *Washington Post*, March 17.
Greenhouse, Steven (1994). "One Aviator Was Killed in North Korea Helicopter Downing," *New York Times*, December 19. Accessed January 16, 2018.
Grohmann, Karolos (2017). "North Korea Crisis So Far No Threat to Pyeongchang 2018: IOC," *reuters.com*, September 11. Accessed December 29, 2017.
Guardian (2008). "US Removes North Korea from Terrorism Blacklist," *theguardian.com*, October 11. Accessed December 16, 2017.
Haas, Michael, ed. (1989). *Korean Reunification: Alternative Pathways*. 1st edn. New York: Praeger.
Haas, Michael, ed. (2012). *Korean Reunification: Alternative Pathways*. 2nd edn. Los Angeles, CA: Publishinghouse for Scholars.
Harris, Gardiner (2017). "Tillerson Hails U.N. Sanctions, as Chinese Minister Rebukes North Korea at ASEAN Meeting," *New York Times*, August 6.
Hastings, Justin V. (2016). *A Most Enterprising Country: North Korea in the Global Economy*. Ithaca, NY: Cornell University Press.
Hecker, Siegfried S., Robert L. Carlin, and Elliot A. Serbin (2018). "A Technically-Informed Roadmap for North Korea's Denuclearization," Center for International Security and Cooperation, Stanford University, May 28.
Hennigan, W. J. (2017). "North Korea Tests Second Powerful Missile This Month," *Los Angeles Times*, July 28.
Hennigen, W. J., David S. Cloud, and Noah Bierman (2017). "'Fire and Fury Like the World Has Never Seen'," *Los Angeles Times*, August 9.
Howard, Peter (2004). "Why Not Invade North Korea? Threats, Language Games, and U.S. Foreign Policy," *International Studies Quarterly*, 48 (4): 805–828.
Kaiman, Jonathan (2017). "N. Korea Says U.S. Isn't Safe," *Los Angeles Times*, August 8.
Kaku, Michio (2012). "Images of North Korean Reactor Hit at Progress of Talks," *International Herald Tribune*, June 10.
Kang, David C. (2003). "International Relations Theory and the Second Korean War," *International Studies Quarterly*, 47 (3): 301–324.

Kaseda, Youshinori (2003). "Japan and the Korean Peace Process." In *The Korean Peace Process and the Four Powers*, eds. Tae-Hwan Kwak and Seung Ho Joo, Chapter 7. Aldershot, UK: Ashgate.

Korean Peninsula Energy Development Organization (2006). "Deputy Director's Statement."

Kerr, David (2005). "The Sino-Russian Partnership and U.S. Policy Toward North Korea: From Hegemony to Concert in Northeast Asia," *International Studies Quarterly*, 49 (4): 411–437.

Kim, Christine (2017). "Pyongyang Calls U.S.–South Korean War Games a Step to Nuclear War," *reuters.com*, August 20.

Kim, Jack, and Kiyoshi Takenaka (2017). "North Korea Threatens to 'Sink' Japan, Reduce U.S. to 'Ashes and Darkness'," *reuters.com*. September 14.

Kim, Stella, and Saphora Smith (2017). North Korea's 'Hostage Diplomacy': Kim Uses Detained Americans as Leverage," *nbcnews.com*, May 8. Accessed August 19, 2017.

Kim, Suzy, and John Feffer (2008). "Hardliners Target Détente with North Korea," *Foreign Policy in Focus*, February 11. *www.fpif.org/fpiftxt/4951*.

Kramer, Gene (1994). "12 Arrested in POW–MIA Rally Outside White House," *Honolulu Advertiser*, July 17: A14.

Krever, Mick, and Joshua Berliner (2017). "UN Official Who Visited Pyongyang Sees 'High Risk' of Miscalculation," *cnn.com*, December 14.

Kristensen, Hans M. (2005). "A History of U.S. Nuclear Weapons in South Korea," *Bulletin of American Scientists*, January 19.

Landler, Mark (2017). "On North Korea, Trump Says Talks Are 'Not the Answer'," *New York Times*, August 31.

Lauren, Paul, Gordon Craig, and Alexander George (2007). *Force and Statecraft: Diplomatic Challenges of Our Time*. New York: Oxford University Press.

Lederer, Edith M. (2017). "UN Security Council Imposes New Sanctions on North Korea," *New York Daily News*, December 22.

Lee Jae-Bong (2008). "U.S. Deployment of Nuclear Weapons in 1950s South Korea & North Korea's Nuclear Development: Toward Denuclearization of the Korean Peninsula," *Asia–Pacific Journal*, 7 (8): 1–17.

Lee Jae-Bong (2012). "The Contemporary Approach to Korean Reunification." In *Korean Reunification: Alternative Pathways*, ed. Michael Haas, 2nd edn, Chapter 9. Los Angeles, CA: Publishinghouse for Scholars.

Lendon, Brad (2017). "North Korea: 3 US Aircraft Carriers Creating 'Worst Ever' Situation," *cnn.com*, November 14. Accessed November 17, 2017.

Lindsay, James M., and Michael E. O'Hannon (2001). *Defending America*. Washington, DC: Brookings.

Litwak, Robert (2000). *Rogue States and United States Foreign Policy*. Princeton, NJ: Woodrow Wilson Center Press.

Litwak, Robert, and Robert Daly (2016). "How to Freeze N. Korea's Nukes," *Los Angeles Times*, May 6.

Lockie, Alex (2017). "China Appears to Have Crossed Trump on North Korea," *aol.com/article/news*, November 16.

Maja, King (2017). "The Greatest Military Exercise in North Korea's History," *us.blastingnews.com*, April 26. Accessed August 3, 2017.

Makinen, Julie, and Steven Borowiec (2016). "US, South Korea Agree to Deploy Anti-Missile System to Counter North," *Los Angeles Times*, July 8.

Manyin, Mark E., and Mary Beth D. Nitikin (2014). "Foreign Assistance to North Korea," *Congressional Research Service*, April 2.

Martin, Gus (2008). *Understanding Terrorism: Challenges, Perspectives and Issues*. 2nd edn. Newbury Park, CA: Sage.

Mathews, Jessica (2017). "Letter to the Editor Response," *New York Review of Books*, 64 (15): 46.

McManus, Doyle (2017). "They Pulled the U.S. Back from the Nuclear Brink," *Los Angeles Times*, August 16.

Meyers, Brian R. (2015). *North Korea's Juche Myth*. Busan: Sthele Press.

Micklethwaite, Jamie (2017). "China Would Step in to Defend North Korea If It Was Attacked by the US, an Ambassador Has Shockingly Claimed," *dailystar.co.uk*, September 14.

Morello, Carol (2017). "US. Sanctions Chinese, Russian Firms, Individuals for Ties to North Korea," *Washington Post*, August 22.

Morello, Carol, and Simon Denyer (2017). "U.S. Calls on All Nations to Sever Ties with North Korea," *Washington Post*, November 29.

Nakamura, David (2017). "Trump Puts North Korea Back on State Sponsors of Terrorism List to Escalate Pressure over Nuclear Weapons," *Washington Post*, November 20.

Nakamura, David, and Carol D. Leonnig (2018). "Trump, South Korean Leader Commiserate over Upcoming Summit," *Washington Post*, May 20.

Nakamura, David, Philip Rucker, Anna Fifield, and Anne Gearan, "Trump-Kim Summit: Trump Says after Historic Meeting, "We Have Developed a Very Special Bond," *Washington Post*, June 12.

New York Times (2017). "In Rare Gesture, North Says It Will Return South Korean Fishing Boat," *New York Times*, October 27.

Noack, Rick (2018). "How Kim-Trump Tensions Escalated: The More the U.S. Said 'Libya,' the Angrier North Korea Got," *Washington Post*, May 24.

Oliphant, James (2018). "Trump Says He Would 'Absolutely' Talk to North Korea's Kim on Phone," *reuters.com*, January 6.

Pape, Robert A. (1997). "Why Economic Sanctions Do Not Work," *International Security*, 22 (2): 90–136.

Pentchoukov, Ivan (2017). "Dennis Rodman Offers to Lead North Korea Talks," *theepochtimes.com*, December 12.

Perlez, Jane (2001). "Powell Says U.S. Wants to Resume Talks with North Korea," *New York Times*, July 28. Accessed December 29, 2017.

Perlez, Jane (2013). "Another American Is Arrested in North Korea," *New York Times*, November 20.

Perlez, Jane, and Yufun Huang (2016). "A Hole in North Korean Sanctions Big Enough for Coal, Oil, and Used Pianos," *New York Times*, March 31.

Pollack, Jonathan H. (2003). "The United States, North Korea, and the End of the Agreed Framework," *Naval War College Review*, 56 (3): 11–49.

PressTV (2017). "China Calls on US, North Korea to Tone Down Rhetoric," *presstv.com*, December 8. Accessed December 29, 2017.

Purefoy, Christian (2007). "Crew Wins Deadly Pirate Battle off Somalia," *cnn.com*, October 30.

Radchenko, Sergey (2011). "Sport and Politics on the Korean Peninsula: North Korea and the 1988 Seoul Olympics," Woodrow Wilson International Center for Scholars, December 12, *wilsoncenter.org*. Accessed January 16, 2018.

Rajaman, Maya (2018). "Putin Says 'Shrewd' Kim Jong Un Has Outwitted Trump in Nuclear Standoff Between North Korea, U.S.," *Newsweek*, January 11.

Reuters (2016). "Korean American Detained in North Korea Was Pastor—Defector," *reuters.com*, January 12. Accessed January 22, 2016.

Rocha, Veronica (2017). "Air Force Launches Test Missile off Central California Coast to Show Nuclear Deterrent Capability," *Los Angeles Times*, April 26.

Sagan, Scott D. (2017). "The Korean Missile Crisis: Why Deterrence Is Still the Best Option," *Foreign Affairs*, 96 (6): 72–82.

Samore, Gary S. (2004). "The Korean Nuclear Crisis," *Survival*, 45 (1): 7–24.

Sanger, David E., and William J. Broad (2017). "Trump Inherits a Secret Cyberwar Against North Korean Missiles," *New York Times*, March 4.

Scanlon, Charles (2007). "The End of a Long Confrontation?," *bbc.com/news*, February 13.

Selden, Mark, and Alvin Y. So (2004). *War and State Terrorism: The United States, Japan, and the Asia-Pacific in the Long Twentieth Century*. Boulder, CO: Rowman & Littlefield.

Shanker, Thom, and Choe Sang-Un (2013). "U.S. Runs Practice Sortie in South Korea," *New York Times*, April 2.

Shenon, Philip (2002). "North Korea Says Nuclear Program Can Be Negotiated," *New York Times*, November 3.

Sigal, Leon V. (1998). *Disarming Strangers: Nuclear Diplomacy with North Korea*. Princeton, NJ: Princeton University Press.

Sigal, Leon V. (2002). "North Korea Is No Iraq: Pyongyang's Negotiating Strategy," *armscontrol.org*. Accessed December 16, 2017.

Slevin, Peter (2002). "N. Korea and U.S. to Meet," *Washington Post*, May 1.

Smith-Spark, Laura, Taehoon Lee, and Catherine Treyz (2017). "US, South Korea Set to Revise Bilateral Missile Treaty," *cnn.com*, September 2.

Solomon, Jay (2017). "North Korea's Top Nuclear Negotiator Held Secret Talks with U.S. Diplomats," *Wall Street Journal*, June 19. Accessed November 29, 2017.

Spetalnick, Matt, and David Brunnstrom (2017). "Despite Tillerson Overture, White House Says Not Right Time for North Korea Talks," *reuters.com*, December 13.

Stanton, Joshua, Sung-Yoon Lee, and Bruce Klingner (2017). "Getting Tough on North Korea: How to Hit Pyongyang Where It Hurts," *Foreign Affairs*, 96 (3): 65–75.

Steuck, William (1995). *The Korean War: An International History*. Princeton, NJ: Princeton University Press.

Stiles, Mary (2017). "South Korea Leader's Antiwar Talk," *Los Angeles Times*, August 18.

Stiles, Mary (2018a). "North Korea's Dictator–Statesmanship?," *Los Angeles Times*, January 6.

Stiles, Mary (2018b). "North Korea's Noteworthy Deal," *Los Angeles Times*, January 16.
United States, Air Force (1979). *A Report on Operation Jilli*. Washington, DC: US Air Force.
United States, Coast Guard (2017). "North Korean Crisis Delays Return of MIA Remains," ngaus.org/newsroom/news/north-korean-crisis-delays, August 19. Accessed August 18, 2017.
United States, Department of Defense, POW/MIA Accounting Agency (2017). "Korean War Accounting," dpaa.mil/Our-Missing/Korean-War. Accessed December 16, 2017.
United States, Department of State (1957). *Modernization of United States Forces in Korea*. Washington, DC: Office of the Historian, U.S. Department of State.
United States, National Guard (2017). "North Korea Crisis Delays Return of MIA Remains," ngaus.org, August 15. Accessed August 18, 2017.
Wagner, John (2018). "Trump Acknowledges He Spoke to Kim Jong Un Before the Singapore Summit," *Washington Post*, June 12.
Washington Post (2009). "Timeline: North Korea's Nuclear Program," *Washington Post*, June 10.
Wikipedia (2017). "Korean Armistice Agreement," wikipedia.com. Accessed August 3, 2017.

Appendix

Table 4.1. American Negotiations with North Korea.

Year	Negative Moves	Year	Positive Moves
1953	USA increases troops, contrary to armistice	1953	USA releases POWs
1953	USA forms alliance with SK	1968	USA stops sending hostile leaflets to NK
1953	USA imposes trade ban on NK	1969	USA removes 1/3 of troops from SK
1955	USA–SK military exercises begin	1989	USA allows NK visitors
1958	USA introduces nuclear weapons into SK	1991	USA withdraws nuclear weapons from SK
1964	USA sends hostile leaflets to NK	1991	USA agrees to allow NK membership in UN
1976	USA doubles troops used in war games with SK	1993	USA begins talks with NK diplomats at UN
1977	Carter revokes pledge to cut troops from SK	1993	USA assures of nonaggression with NK
1983	USA refuses to pull out nuclear weapons	1993	USA promises NK never to threaten force
1983	USA refuses to discuss denuclearization with NK	1993	USA promises noninterference with NK internal affairs

(Continued)

Table 4.1. (*Continued*)

Year	Negative Moves	Year	Positive Moves
1988	USA lists NK as state sponsor of terrorism	1994	USA accepts NK offer to negotiate
1992	USA imposes new sanctions on NK	1994	USA promises eventual normalization
1993	USA gets UNSC to impose sanctions	1994	USA accepts Agreed Framework with NK
1993	USA: IAEA inspection clearance before normalization talks	1994	USA promises heavy fuel oil for NK power
1993	USA threatens to put Patriot missiles into SK	1995	USA cancels military exercises with SK
1994	USA puts Patriot missiles into SK	1996	USA cancels military exercises with SK
1994	USA threatens war with NK	1996	USA removes NK from list of "rogue states"
1995	USA begins delays of fuel oil shipments to NK	1998	USA sends food to NK
1995	USA begins delays of light-water reactor to NK	1999	USA open for normalization talks if NK will provide security guarantee
1997	USA resumes military exercises with SK	1999	USA offers to lift sanctions if NK ends missile development and sales
1997	USA imposes sanctions on NK	1999	USA eases NK economic restrictions
1998	USA imposes sanctions on NK	2000	USA lifts some sanctions from NK
1999	USA threatens more sanctions on NK	2000	U.S. Secretary of State promises peace talks
2000	USA reimposes sanctions on NK	2001	U.S. Secretary of State offers negotiations without preconditions
2000	USA rejects NK offer to halt missile development	2002	U.S. Secretary of State praises NK compliance with Agreed Framework
2001	USA reimposes sanctions on NK	2003	USA agrees to Six-Party Talks

Year	Negative Moves	Year	Positive Moves
2001	USA cancels oil shipments to NK	2003	USA pledges peaceful coexistence with NK
2002	Bush cancels Agreed Framework	2003	USA agrees to security guarantee with NK short of a nonaggression pact
2002	Bush revokes promised negotiations with NK	2005	USA accepts NK sovereignty
2002	US imposes new sanctions on NK	2005	USA reaffirms pledge never to attack NK
2002	Axis of Evil speech	2005	USA accepts NK right of peaceful nuclear power
2002	USA stops fuel oil delivery to NK	2005	USA pledges increased economic cooperation
2002	Bush threatens nuclear strike on NK	2005	USA OKs bilateral talks with NK
2003	USA new precondition to talks: denuclearization	2006	USA promises partial unfreezing of NK assets
2003	USA opposes nonaggression pact with NK	2007	USA agrees to normalization talks
2003	USA opposes bilateral talks with NK	2007	USA pledges to stop calling NK a terrorist state
2003	USA reimposes sanctions on NK	2007	USA sends more humanitarian aid to NK
2003	USA initiates Proliferation Security Initiative	2007	USA pledges to ship more heavy fuel oil to NK
2004	USA denies NK right of peaceful nuclear power	2007	USA pledges to negotiate peace with NK
2005	U.S. official Rice: NK is "outpost of tyranny"	2007	USA ships more heavy fuel oil to NK
2005	USA imposes new sanctions on NK	2007	U.S. military aids North Koreans caught by Somali pirates
2005	USA refuses to unfreeze NK assets	2007	USA promises to end NK sanctions
2005	USA revokes permission to allow NK to develop peaceful uses of nuclear power	2007	USA promises humanitarian aid to NK

(*Continued*)

Table 4.1. (Continued)

Year	Negative Moves	Year	Positive Moves
2005	USA imposes new demands re NK human rights	2008	USA removes NK from list of states sponsoring terrorism
2006	USA stops humanitarian aid to NK	2008	New York Philharmonic plays in Pyongyang
2006	USA reimposes sanctions on NK	2009	USA sends food to NK
2006	USA admits freezing NK assets for bargaining	2009	USA proposes talks with NK
2006	USA ends promise to supply light-water reactor to NK	2012	USA resumes food aid to NK
2007	USA suspends shipment of heavy fuel oil to NK	2017	USA pledges no regime change for NK
2007	USA makes demands on NK outside of Six-Party Talks: inspections all over NK	2017	USA pledges negotiations, not war, if missile tests stop
2007	USA refuses talks with NK on normalization	2017	USA opens back-channel negotiations with NK
2008	USA revokes promise to remove NK from list of states sponsoring terrorism	2018	USA postpones military exercises scheduled for February
2009	Obama welches promise to meet NK leader	2018	U.S. president indicates interest in direct telephone call with NK leader
2009	USA condemns NK satellite launch	2018	U.S. president denies that a preemptive strike is being planned
2009	USA condemns NK nuclear test	2018	U.S. president agrees to meet NK leader
2009	USA stops sending food to NK	2018	U.S. president describes NK leader as "honorable"
2009	USA reimposes sanctions on NK	2018	U.S. president considers removing troops from SK
2009	U.S. officials say "all options are on the table"	2018	U.S. war games toned down in March and April
2010	USA refuses to attend Six-Party Talks	2018	U.S. president assures no regime change for NK
2011	new USA precondition to normalization talks: denuclearization evidence	2018	U.S. CIA head and Secretary of State make 2 visits to NK

Year	Negative Moves	Year	Positive Moves
2012	USA gets UN sanctions on NK	2018	U.S. president keeps door open for a summit after cancellation
2013	USA gets UN sanctions on NK	2018	U.S. president and secretary of state promise economic aid
2013	USA stops sending food to NK	2018	U.S. president meets NK leader at summit, makes 4 pledges
2013	USA has B-2 bomber fly around Korea	2018	U.S. hints that war games will stop someday
2014	USA refuses to accept NK peace treaty offer		
2015	USA precondition to normalization or peace talks: denuclearization		
2016	USA cyberwar on NK		
2016	USA imposes more sanctions on NK		
2016	USA gets more UN sanctions on NK		
2016	USA brings back nuclear weapons to war games		
2016	USA war games include plot to kill NK leader		
2016	USA deploys anti-missile system hinted in 2009		
2016	USA puts NK leader on sanctions list		
2017	USA rejects China's plea to negotiate with NK		
2017	Trump welches on promise to meet NK leader		
2017	USA closes back-channel with NK at UN		
2017	USA ends Obama policy of strategic patience		
2017	USA new policy appears to be an attack on NK when an unspecified "red line" is crossed		

(Continued)

Table 4.1. (*Continued*)

Year	Negative Moves	Year	Positive Moves
2017	USA sends warships toward NK		
2017	USA gets more UN sanctions against NK		
2017	U.S. Congress passes additional NK sanctions		
2017	Trump makes acerbic comments about NK		
2017	USA sends B-1s and B-2s near NK		
2017	USA sends F-45 fighter jets near NK		
2017	U.S. president opposes diplomacy		
2017	USA war games include plot to kill NK leader		
2017	U.S. president says war is one option		
2017	USA allows SK to develop longer-range missiles		
2017	USA threatens trade war with China and others doing business with NK		
2017	USA president insults NK leader		
2017	US president threatens that the NK leader "will not be around much longer"		
2017	USA engages a second set of war games involving 3 aircraft carriers, B-1 bombers		
2017	USA deploys F-35 stealth fighter jets		
2017	USA rejects China proposal for a freeze on NK tests along with an end to USA war games		
2017	USA puts NK on list of states sponsoring terrorism		

Year	Negative Moves	Year	Positive Moves
2017	USA calls on all countries to cut commercial and diplomatic ties with NK		
2017	USA bans all travel by Americans to NK		
2018	USA president harshly criticizes NK leader		
2018	U.S. adviser threatens to impose Libyan model on NK		
2018	USA introduces nuclear-capable warplanes into SK, some in May war games simulating attack on NK		
2018	U.S. vice president reiterates Libyan model for NK		
2018	U.S. president cancels summit		

Table 4.2. North Korean Negotiations with the United States.

Year	Negative Moves	Year	Positive Moves
1953	NK increases troops, contrary to armistice	1953	NK releases POWs
1953	NK demand to NNSC: stop inspections	1953	NK begins to return MIAs
1958	NK army masses along DMZ border	1971	NK allows US travelers
1961	NK signs alliances with PRC and USSR	1974	NK first proposes peace treaty
1966	NK armed infiltration into SK	1983	NK offers to abandon nuclear power
1968	NK seizes USS *Pueblo*	1983	NK first proposes normalization with USA
1969	NK shoots down U.S. spy plane	1983	NK joins NPT
1972	NK stops American travelers	1983	NK first admits IAEA inspectors
1977	NK bombs SK jet	1986	NK readmits IAEA inspectors
1983	NK fails to sign IAEA safeguards agreement	1988	NK supports Olympic Games in Korea

(*Continued*)

Table 4.2. (*Continued*)

Year	Negative Moves	Year	Positive Moves
1984	NK launches missile	1989	IAEA: NK in full compliance with NPT
1986	NK blocks IAEA inspectors temporarily	1991	NK signs denuclearization declaration with SK
1990	NK tests a missile that fails	1991	NK signs IAEA safeguards agreement
1991	NK successfully tests a missile	1992	NK admits IAEA inspectors again
1992	NK sells missiles to Pakistan	1993	NK promises to abandon nuclear program
1993	NK conducts four missile tests	1993	NK withdraws threat to pull out of NPT
1993	NK threatens to withdraw from NPT	1993	NK admits IAEA inspectors again
1993	NK refuses entry to IAEA inspectors	1994	NK admits IAEA inspectors again
1993	NK expels Czechs from NNSC	1994	NK accepts offer of USA to negotiate
1994	NK hides nuclear fuel rods from inspectors	1994	NK accepts light-water reactor to replace nuclear reactor
1994	NK threatens to pull out of IAEA	1994	NK invites Jimmy Carter for talks
1994	NK withdraws from MAC	1994	NK accepts Agreed Framework agreement
1994	NK shoots down U.S. airplane	1994	NK agrees to abandon nuclear power
1995	NK expels Poles from NNSC	1994	NK accepts precondition of IAEA inspection clearance before normalization
1996	NK ships missiles to Iran	1994	NK agrees to store spent nuclear fuel rods
1996	NK arrests first American citizen	1994	NK agrees to can spent nuclear fuel rods
1998	NK launches satellite, missiles	1994	NK agrees to freeze nuclear program
1998	NK stops canning nuclear rods	1994	NK agrees to dismantle nuclear program upon receipt of the light-water reactor

Year	Negative Moves	Year	Positive Moves
1998	NK threat to develop nuclear weapons	1994	NK promises to remain in NPT
2001	NK ships missiles to Iran	1994	NK promises to admit past violations after receipt of light-water reactor
2001	NK expels IAEA inspectors	1994	NK releases captured pilot and body of dead pilot
2002	NK threatens nuclear war with USA	1995	IAEA: 3 NK nuclear facilities not operational
2002	NK naval battle with SK	1996	NK agrees to limit missile development
2002	NK ships nuclear material	1996	NK releases detained American citizen
2003	NK ships missiles to Pakistan	1999	NK moratorium on missile tests begins
2003	NK admits restarting nuclear program	1999	NK admits IAEA inspectors
2003	NK expels IAEA inspectors	1999	IAEA: no cheating by NK
2003	NK intercepts U.S. spy plane in Sea of Japan	2000	NK offers to end missile program
2003	NK threatens test of nuclear weapons	2001	NK offers to end nuclear program
2003	NK boycotts Six-Party talks	2002	NK offers to stop missile development
2005	NK boycotts Six-Party talks	2003	NK offers to denuclearize after normalization
2005	NK conducts missile tests	2003	NK agrees to Six-Party Talks
2005	NK threatens to give nuclear weapons to terrorists	2003	NK returns to Six-Party Talks
2006	NK conducts first nuclear weapons test	2004	NK offers to dismantle all nuclear weapons
2006	NK conducts 7 missile tests	2004	NK pledges peaceful coexistence with SK, USA
2007	NK boycotts Six-Party talks	2004	NK proposes denuclearized Korean peninsula

(Continued)

Table 4.2. (Continued)

Year	Negative Moves	Year	Positive Moves
2008	NK restarts main nuclear reactor	2005	NK returns to Six-Party Talks
2008	NK restarts nuclear weapons program	2005	NK pledges to dismantle all nuclear weapons
2008	NK turns away IAEA inspectors	2005	NK pledges to rejoin NPT
2008	NK naval battle with SK	2005	NK pledges to allow IAEA inspection
2009	NK naval battle with SK	2006	NK promises to freeze nuclear weapons program
2009	NK stops going to Panmunjom for talks	2006	NK pledges "no first use" of nuclear weapons
2009	NK launches satellite, eight missile tests	2007	NK promises to shut down main nuclear reactor
2009	NK pulls out of Six-Party Talks	2007	NK promises to allow IAEA inspectors
2009	NK arrests 3 American citizens	2007	IAEA: NK's main nuclear reactor is shut down
2010	NK naval battle with SK	2007	NK promises to tell all about nuclear program
2012	NK launches satellite, missile tests	2007	NK shuts down main nuclear reactor
2013	NK conducts nuclear weapons test	2007	NK returns to Six-Party Talks
2013	NK renounces nonaggression pact with SK	2007	NK signs denuclearization pledge
2013	NK cuts direct telephone tie with SK	2008	NK renounces terrorist actions
2013	NK makes first threat to attack USA	2008	NK promises to tell all about nuclear program
2013	NK on rocket alert after missile tests	2008	NK releases 18,000 pages about nuclear program
2013	NK new precondition to ending nuclear program: withdrawal of U.S. troops from SK	2008	New York Philharmonic plays in Pyongyang

Year	Negative Moves	Year	Positive Moves
2013	NK restarts main nuclear reactor	2009	NK invites IAEA inspectors
2013	NK arrests 1 American citizen	2009	NK releases 2 American hostages
2014	NK arrests 1 American citizen	2010	NK releases 1 American hostage
2014	NK cyberattacks U.S. film studio	2011	NK agrees to return to Six-Party Talks
2014	NK conducts more missile tests	2011	NK freezes nuclear weapons program
2014	NK conducts many rounds of rocket firing	2011	NK suspends nuclear enrichment
2014	NK shells SK	2011	NK invites IAEA inspectors
2014	NK threatens another nuclear test	2011	NK offers moratorium on all testing
2015	NK conducts more missile tests	2012	NK declares moratorium on nuclear enrichment
2015	NK conducts another nuclear test	2012	NK declares moratorium on missile testing
2015	NK arrests 1 American citizen	2012	NK invites IAEA inspectors
2016	NK launches another satellite	2012	NK calls for return of Six-Party Talks
2016	NK arrests 1 American citizen	2013	NK releases American citizen
2016	NK threatens nuclear war with USA	2013	NK calls for peace treaty with USA
2016	NK H-bomb test + another	2013	NK welcomes Dennis Rodman
2016	NK precondition to denuclearization: peace treaty	2014	NK welcomes Dennis Rodman
2016	NK stops using UN back-channel with USA	2014	NK releases 3 American hostages
2016	NK installs mines along DMZ	2015	NK offers to suspend nuclear tests
2016	NK conducts 24 missile tests	2016	NK agrees to talk about denuclearization
2017	NK arrests 2 American citizens	2016	NK proposes peace treaty
2017	NK leader makes acerbic comments	2017	NK promises no nuclear war with Japan or SK

(Continued)

Table 4.2. (*Continued*)

Year	Negative Moves	Year	Positive Moves
2017	NK declares denuclearization impossible	2017	NK welcomes Dennis Rodman
2017	NK threatens to send missiles near Guam	2017	NK releases 1 American hostage
2017	NK threatens war with Japan, USA	2017	NK cancels Guam threat
2017	NK tests 17 medium-range missiles, 2 over Japan	2017	NK promises to freeze its nuclear program if negotiations proceed toward a peace treaty
2017	NK tests 3 ICBMs, one with a range that might hit the East Coast of the USA	2017	NK returns boat and crew of SK vessel detained in NK waters
2017	NK conducts a second H-bomb test	2017	NK promises to freeze its missile and nuclear tests if the USA will stop war games
2017	NK leader insults U.S. leader	2017	NK stops missile/nuclear tests for 74 days
2017	NK foreign minister says bombing USA is "inevitable"	2018	NK continues to stop missile/nuclear tests
2017	NK threatens to shoot down U.S. warplanes outside its airspace	2018	NK leader offers to meet Trump
2018	NK leader taunts U.S. leader with his nuclear deterrent	2018	NK hints denuclearization
2018	NK cancels talks with SK	2018	NK agrees to denuclearization
2018	NK rejects USA "blackmail"	2018	NK does not object to USA war games
2018	NK rejects Libyan model, attacking USA vice president as a "dummy"	2018	NK hosts high-level USA emissary
		2018	NK releases 3 American prisoners
		2018	NK talks reluctant U.S. president into attending the summit
		2018	NK leader signs Singapore Declaration
		2018	NK agrees to destroy a missile site

PART 3

IMPLICATIONS

The need for normal relations between countries is obvious, lest war will disturb the world. Theories about how to bring about normalization, as identified in Chapter 2, now need to be tested with information derived from the case studies of American negotiations with North Korea and Vietnam. Implications for future situations flow from the analysis.

Accordingly, the final chapter presents tests based on major paradigms of international studies and political science. The conclusions suggest improvements in American diplomacy that may startle many readers in the United States Department of State and elsewhere.

· 5 ·

CONCLUSIONS BASED ON ALTERNATIVE PARADIGMS

Two puzzles were initially posed. The question of how to get former enemies to the bargaining table is much easier than the question about how bargaining can produce normalization of commercial and diplomatic relations.

Four theories, which are paradigms because they have applicability beyond the question of normalization, were posed in Chapter 2. Now is the time to determine which fit the two cases described in Chapters 3 and 4 and to draw conclusions that will serve to encourage better pathways toward normalization of relations between countries throughout the world.

Deterrence Paradigm

According to the Deterrence Paradigm, power should be the key element explaining success in normalization. The United States, more powerful than both North Korea and Vietnam, should presumably have prevailed in any negotiations.

The first prediction is that two rival countries with relative equality in power will normalize relations when a third country emerges as a threat to both. But the United States remains stronger than both North Korea and Vietnam, so the prediction does not apply. The rise of China might be considered as that third country for both the United States and Vietnam, but normalization occurred after Chinese attacks on Vietnam during the 1980s and before China claimed sovereignty over islands in the South China Sea. Hanoi and Washington have common interests regarding Chinese expansionism, but by the time Vietnam's counterclaims were in jeopardy, relations with the United States had already been normalized.

North Korea's best friends today are China and Russia. Neither the United States nor the DPRK have experienced a third country threat to drive them to the bargaining table.

The second prediction is that when one country in a bilateral relationship becomes weaker, then that country will concede to terms dictated by the stronger. The record of negotiations indeed demonstrates that the United States would not discuss normalization with Vietnam until the latter's troops were out of Cambodia and the alliance with the Soviet Union was defunct. Nevertheless, confidence-building measures were undertaken on less strategic matters, starting with the issue of MIAs.

Whereas China and the Soviet Union backed North Korea during the Cold War, Pyongyang was considerably isolated and weakened when the Cold War ended. Accordingly, the DPRK's requests for normalization and a peace treaty fell on deaf ears in Washington. North Korea made repeated concessions to the United States, but in vain, so the pursuit of nuclear power was an effort to level the warring field. The United States then became interested in negotiating as North Korea gained strength. Washington could have easily stopped Pyongyang's nuclear developments by agreeing to a peace treaty and achieving normalization in relations; the tradeoff was obvious. Why Washington failed to do so is a major puzzle that can only be explained by the possibility that South Korea tried to veto such a détente. In 1998, when President Kim Dae Jung became president, and North–South relations improved, President George W. Bush inexplicably stopped progress with an ill-advised Axis of Evil speech in 2002.

The logic of deterrence cannot explain the fact that the United States allowed North Korea to develop a nuclear deterrent, making the power relationship more equal. Washington considered (in deterrence logic) that China played a dominant role over Pyongyang and would rein in its neighbor. Were Pyongyang totally isolated and in fear of Beijing, then Washington might seek normalization with North Korea based on deterrence logic. Instead, Beijing refused to abandon an ally and thereby weaken its own dominant role in Northeast Asia. Another war in Korea would not serve China's interest, and the best way for Beijing to deter the United States from a reckless preemptive strike was to allow North Korea to gain some deterrent capability. The DPRK would never be so foolish as to launch an attack, knowing the superior military capability of the United States.

The logic of the Deterrence Paradigm suggests that nuclear North Korea and the United States had no choice but to engage in mutual deterrence. In due course, the United States was predicted by deterrence logic to settle down and treat Pyongyang on a more equal basis. Normalization of relations and a peace treaty now mutually serves to lessen tensions, just as Washington treads lightly with nuclear powers China and Russia. After all, China and Russia are expansionistic, whereas North Korea is not.

In short, the predictions of the Deterrence Paradigm are not fully borne out by the two case studies. Something beside deterrence logic has operated to explain why normalization occurred more easily in one case rather than the other, leaving three alternative paradigms to investigate.

Selectorate Paradigm

The Deterrence Paradigm assumes that foreign policy decisions are made entirely on the basis of exogenous factors—the relative power positions between two countries. The Selectorate Paradigm instead focuses on societal factors—changes in leaders, economic realities, and political regime types.

Leadership Changes

Government heads seek to remain in office as long as possible, so they view external events as potential threats to their domestic power positions. One key factor in the Selectorate Paradigm is whether leaders are Doves or Hawks. Doves are predicted to be the most interested in peace but the most vulnerable to domestic opposition when they make concessions to other countries. The prediction based on leadership change is that successful negotiations ensue when Hawks replace Doves and then proceed toward normalization, provided that the Hawks offer payoffs in the form of private or public goods.

In the case of Vietnam, the peace treaty of 1973 came after Nixon, having been hawkish for four years, was re-elected in 1972 with a dovish promise to end the war. Presumably Nixon sought to use his political capital for such a popular decision during his final term in office, but a scandal erupted, and he resigned in

1974. His successor, Gerald Ford, did not distinguish himself as either a Dove or a Hawk, but he was defeated in 1976 by dovish Jimmy Carter, who in turn tried to pave the way for normalization until he considered that Vietnam's entry into Cambodia in 1978 precluded any more conciliatory steps. Hawk Ronald Reagan maintained opposition to Hanoi's role in Cambodia throughout his eight years in office; nevertheless, his policy regarding MIAs distributed some rewards to affected families. President George H.W. Bush, who succeeded Reagan, was so hawkish that he blundered at the Paris conference on Cambodia in 1989. The peace agreement of 1991 was forced upon him by allies. Dovish Bill Clinton, elected in 1992, accomplished normalization, providing such rewards for American businesses as offshore petroleum exploration.

Dovish American presidents Carter and Clinton made the most progress toward normalization with North Korea, but Dove Obama missed every opportunity to do so. The other presidents were hawkish and often drove their counterparts in Pyongyang to even more hawkish positions. American Hawks refused to recognize that the prime dovish goals of North Korea have remained normalization and peace. On many occasions, the DPRK made concessions, dropped preconditions, and tried to demonstrate good faith. But when hawkish Washington backtracked, raised suspicions, or protested about something without first dealing with issues quietly, North Korea overresponded with hawkish behavior.

Consistent with another study (Fehrs 2016:Table2b), the Hawk–Dove role analysis, in other words, does not provide a consistent explanation for the ups and downs of diplomacy success and failure. Nevertheless, American cooperation with Vietnam did yield bilateral benefits to businesses, immigrants, and tourists. No such benefits were anticipated or resulted from contact between North Korea and the United States, though Trump raised the possibility of a Trump hotel on a tourist-oriented beach resort during the Singapore summit. Thus, the public goods element is part of the explanation for success in the case of Vietnam and for failure regarding North Korea.

Economic Change

The second Selectorate scenario predicts that normalization of relations is more likely when a country opens its economy to the possibility of private and public goods payoffs. Both North Korea and Vietnam have indeed changed their economic systems from rigid socialism. Vietnam maintains state control over parts of the economy today but the private sector began to surge about the time when normalization talks were making progress (World Bank 2017), thereby providing public goods to increase public support within the United States. North Korea perfunctorily transitioned from state socialism to state capitalism in the 1990s, following the Chinese model, but remained committed to economic autonomy and smuggling, which benefits DPRK leaders as private goods and offers nothing to American entrepreneurs. After Kim Jong Un succeeded his father in 2011, considerably more capitalist enterprises arose, and the economy began to exhibit prosperity in the capital city.

In short, there appears to be a correlation: Economic changes in Vietnam were associated with progress leading to normalization, while failure to experience major economic changes in North Korea until very recently coincided with a lack of progress in diplomacy. But the correlation seems spurious because both Asian countries sought normalization all along; their economic changes did not compel a new foreign policy. United States policy responded positively to Hanoi much more than Pyongyang, and the fact that the former changed more economically than the latter seems consistent with the Selectorate Paradigm.

The economic scenario predicted by the Selectorate Paradigm depicts a sharp difference before and after a major change in the nature of an economic system. For Hanoi, the "Hungarian" reforms adopted in Vietnam around the end of the Cold War coincided with announcements about PAVN's withdrawal from Cambodia. But the latter event served to accelerate normalization negotiations, not the economic changes.

In the case of North Korea, concessions were more numerous when Pyongyang was economically weak compared to the present. However, the increased prosperity resulting from the adoption of reforms did not make Pyongyang more conciliatory. Instead, the DPRK's increased wealth served to finance the development in missiles and nuclear technologies, which in turn hindered progress with the United States. The logic behind sanctions on North Korea—to inflict so much economic pain that the DPRK will surrender a deterrent capability which the country has long struggled to build—ignored the fact that the arsenal already exists, no longer needing a massive input of national wealth on the part of a country that has been accustomed to hard times.

Democratization

The third Selectorate scenario predicts a greater willingness to normalize relations when a country changes from authoritarian to democratic rule. No such change has occurred in the case of either North Korea or Vietnam.

Implications

In sum, the Selectorate Paradigm asks good questions about how normalization might progress. But the answers fall short.

Mass Society Paradigm

The role of public opinion is central to the Mass Society Paradigm, though not all countries are democratic. The main prediction is that governments achieve normalization only when the masses, as represented by civil society, are in favor. If there is no strong public interest on an issue, governments will do what they believe to be in the national interest.

One clear difference between negotiations involving North Korea and Vietnam is regarding pressures from civil society on Washington (cf. Trumbore 1998). American oil companies were eager to resume exploration along Vietnam's coastline, and they lost out when European oil companies were granted permission by Hanoi. Vietnamese Americans wanted to send money to their relatives, so arrangements required concessions from Washington. There was also a measure of guilt over the unpopular war within some American leaders. John McCain and veterans' organizations wanted an accounting of MIAs and also pressed for normalization when they realized that Vietnam was fully cooperative. Public opinion, thus, played a significant role in encouraging negotiations.

But few such internal pressures have operated in regard to North Korea. Concessions emerged when Washington sent food for starving North Koreans, but that need fluctuated based on the state of North Korean agriculture each year. There is no equivalent to Senator John McCain to serve as a leader in Congress on behalf of solutions to the conflict with the DPRK. With the exception of the New York Philharmonic, some journalists, and tourists who risk arrest, few Americans have any experience in North Korea, and they have not sufficiently mounted a campaign to achieve normalization.

Community Building Paradigm

Whereas the Deterrence Paradigm considers exogenous influences to be primary, the Selectorate Paradigm focuses on societal elements, and the Mass Society Paradigm considers the will of the people, the Community Building

Paradigm spotlights interpersonal communications. A mark of successful diplomacy is when opposite sides enjoy their work because those around the table respect one another. The Community Building Paradigm predicts that progress occurs when contact is enjoyable rather than unpleasant, agreeable rather than distasteful.

The first prediction of the Community Building Paradigm is that countries previously in conflict must change their policies before diplomacy will be undertaken for normalization. Clearly that hurdle was overcome in the case of the United States and Vietnam when the People's Army of Vietnam left Cambodia. Pyongyang began to seek normalization and a peace treaty as early as 1955, but Washington showed no interest in either prospect until the Clinton administration.

The next prediction is that competent diplomats will be assigned to negotiations. Even before PAVN marched out of Cambodia, General John Vessey, Jr., and Foreign Minister Nguyễn Cơ Thạch demonstrated flexibility and sincerity. With the exception of former UN Ambassador Bill Richardson, Washington's negotiators have never praised a North Korean diplomat whom they liked; even armistice negotiations were difficult (Bailey 1992). North Korean diplomats have had a habit of restating rigid positions many times and then unexpectedly making dramatic concessions without demonstrating the skill of compromise. Leaders of the DRPK had a preference for a meeting with the president of the United States as the signal that the war is over and the time for peace is nigh, whereupon the task of drawing up the appropriate documents would be left to those down the two chains of command. That occasion nearly arrived in 2000, but Clinton demurred because he felt that his presence was needed in Washington while the results of the election that year were in doubt, whereas innovative Trump seized the opportunity in 2018.

A corollary of the prediction about competent diplomats is that the need for mediation is an indication that two countries have less diplomatic skills in bilateral negotiations. China volunteered to mediate, as isolated North Korea had little experience in diplomacy. But, consistent with earlier studies (Bercovitch and Jackson 1997; Bercovitch and Gartner 2006; Ghosn 2010), Beijing's mediation with North Korea was unsuccessful; the Six-Party talks broke down.

The third prediction is that confidence-building measures, within or outside the negotiations, will assure success in diplomacy. Having formerly been enemies, there must be clear assurance that one country is not trying to trick the other.

Appendices to Chapters 3 and 4 provide the basis for an estimated count of such positive and negative moves (Table 5.1). Although each item is given a count of one, some are repeated in more than one year. More than a dozen missile tests in 2017, for example, could be contrasted with complex moves in American war games during each of fifty years.

Another complication with the tabulation is that the United States has reported cheating by North Korea on several occasions. In several cases, the report was proved false. Two launches of communication satellites were interpreted as cheating by Washington, but Pyongyang argued that no agreement was literally violated thereby. The alleged cheating in 2003 came after the DPRK felt cheated by Washington that a light-water reactor had been promised in 1994 but had never been delivered. Distrust and suspicion might have been mitigated through increased diplomatic interaction, but the narrative presented in Chapter 4 validates the overall count.

The Community Building Paradigm clearly explains the disparate patterns between North Korea and Vietnam. DPRK–USA negotiations demonstrate a more conciliatory Pyongyang than Washington, but one difficulty has been that hostage taking as well as missile and nuclear testing, designed by North Korea to provoke negotiations leading to normalization of relations, instead prompted the United States to react in a very hostile manner until they reached the brink of war in 2017, SRV–USA negotiations had reversals but still yielded positive results for both sides.

Table 5.1. Positive and Negative Moves During Negotiations.

| | DPRK–USA negotiations || SRV–USA negotiations ||
	United States	North Korea	United States	Socialist Republic of Vietnam
Positive	64	97	39	37
Negative	101	93	21	10
Difference	−37	+4	+18	+27

Source: See Tables 3.1, 3.2, 4.1, 4.2.

The fourth prediction is that private or public benefits will be derived from normalization. Using the eight major values of Harold Lasswell (1951:11), the results indicate payoffs provided by the United States to North Korea and Vietnam during negotiations as a preview of what would occur after normalization (Table 5.2). What is clear is that Vietnam received much more payoff than North Korea.

Table 5.2. Fulfillment of Basic Values Before and During Negotiations.

Value	Example	Vietnam	North Korea
Power	Military	Search for MIAs	Nuclear inspections
Respect	Summits	Foreign minister talks	Foreign minister talks, summit conference
Rectitude	Treaties	Geneva agreement	Armistice
Affection	Resettlement	Out-migration OK	Repatriation only in 1953
Wealth	Trade, travel, etc.	Banking, travel OK	Limited travel
Well-being	Health	Medical equipment	Food aid
Skill	Technical assistance	How to use med equipment	Promise to supply light-water reactors
Enlightenment	Schooling	Scholar/student exchange	Scholar exchange

Source: Chapters 3–4.

Summary

Each of the four paradigms suggests insights, but the Community Building Paradigm is the best predictor. The Deterrence Paradigm predicted that weaker countries would make concessions to stronger countries, but evidence herein is that the stronger country accepted concessions as an invitation for successful negotiations in one case but not the other until very recently. The rise of Vietnam in power projection provoked a failure to negotiate until troops left Cambodia. Increased North Korean military capabilities, demonstrated by testing missiles and nuclear weapons, decreased serious negotiations until North Korea felt confident of a deterrent. In short, the Deterrence Paradigm must be rejected as an unreliable explanation.

Contrary to the Selectorate Paradigm on changes in leadership, Dove leaders in the United States were more successful than Hawks in regard to both North Korea and Vietnam, though Trump changed from hawk to dove, astonishing both opponents and supporters. One reason could be that Hanoi became more dovish, while successive leaders in Pyongyang have been more hawkish, but that fact also contradicts the Selectorate Paradigm. There were more American domestic payoffs regarding Hanoi than Pyongyang, but Doves were responsible, not Hawks.

The Selectorate Paradigm also predicts that fundamental changes in economic and political systems will bring formerly recalcitrant countries to the bargaining table. On the contrary, economic changes designed by the two countries had little impact on normalization negotiations. And neither country became a democracy.

The Mass Society Paradigm successfully predicted that progress toward normalization occurs when civil society exerts pressures on governments. Contrariwise, lacking civil society interest, normalization negotiations fail to sustain any momentum. Nevertheless, the Mass Society Paradigm does not deal with how diplomats will be able to carry out the wishes of the public. Success in diplomacy is best explained by the Community Building Paradigm.

The Community Building paradigm correctly predicted a change in policies to get to the bargaining table—for Vietnam, withdrawal from Cambodia, whereas for North Korea the nuclear buildup produced more interest in sanctions spearheaded by Washington. Thereafter, confidence-building measures during lengthy negotiations built trust with Hanoi as well as Pyongyang (Table 5.1). Confidence-building measures included rewards for both countries, but much more concretely for Vietnam (Table 5.2). A similar effort to cross-test paradigms, though with a different theoretical vocabulary, reached the same conclusion regarding North Korea (Howard 2004).

Clearly, the Community Building Paradigm best fits the profile of how negotiations limped along endogenously, with steps forward and backward. The other paradigms are too removed from the reality of ongoing negotiations during which issues raised by those paradigms had to be surmounted. Details inside the black box, long neglected by scholars seeking to establish the validity of superficial paradigms that assume bivariate models of cross-sectional relations, reveal the actual cross-temporal dynamics.

In addition, leaders varied in their learning curves during the process of normalization. Newly appointed negotiators (Thạch, Vessey, Carter, Clinton) were sometimes needed to put negotiations back on track. North Korean leaders, frustrated at their isolation, appeared unable to understand how to promote constructive diplomacy until Swiss-educated Kim Jong Un demonstrated considerable skill in communications during 2018. When negotiations with Vietnam stalled, unilateral positive concessions got talks back to the bargaining table. For Pyongyang, aggressive moves outside diplomacy were the tactics used to provoke talks, but they did not always work. Whereas the Asian custom of gift-giving upon entry to the home of another person may be equivalent to a confidence-building measure, Pyongyang did not practice that art at the international level on a par with Vietnam until Kim surprised the world in 2018. Washington understood the need for reciprocation to achieve progress but found DPRK aggressive moves intolerable. Positive metacommunication between the Americans and Vietnamese was achieved in the Thạch–Vessey encounters, whereas Kim so impressed Trump with his sincerity that the Singapore summit was scheduled and succeeded.

Some backtracking occurred in U.S.–Vietnam relations, but the deviation from the line of progress in the case of North Korean–United States reversals was considerably disproportionate. North Korea did not take negotiations between lower-level diplomats seriously, being "rank conscious," according to former American ambassador Donald Gregg (Sun 2006:89). Thus, when the American president met the South Korean president in 2001 but not his counterpart in the North, Pyongyang was offended and refused to attend the Six-Party talks (ibid., 110). Indeed, the American desire to coordinate with South Korea often provoked negative responses from Pyongyang, which interpreted the failure to be treated equally as a sign of flagrant disrespect (Snyder 1999). Trump, often criticized at home, was treated with such respect by Kim that he reciprocated, undertook confidence-building measures, and gained a new friend even before they met in Singapore. What Trump doubtless learned as well is that North Korea never wanted nuclear weapons in the first place; they had been frustrated by the United States in seeking normalization of relations and peace since the 1950s.

Conclusion

The analysis herein has achieved the goal of showing how two countries may or may not normalize their diplomatic relations. Although such factors as their power relations, leadership propensities, and domestic pressures are important in initiating and sustaining progress toward normalization, the critical element is how negotiations are conducted—that is, how unilateral reciprocated confidence-building measures can overcome numerous issues in mutual contention.

A similar detailed analysis for other instances of nonrecognition may not necessarily follow the same pattern. The cases of normalization between the United States and Cuba, China, and the Soviet Union have not yet been analyzed with such specificity. More research will establish whether the Community Building Paradigm suggests measures that will assure progress in the goal of transforming conflictual to normal relations between countries around the world.

Meanwhile, the consequences of different paths toward North Korea and Vietnam are evident today. The United States has been invited to return to its former wartime base at Cam Ranh Bay while the outbreak of World War III on the Korean peninsula appears to have been avoided by astute diplomacy. Nevertheless, North Korea and the United States may on the same page today, seeking denuclearization of the Korean peninsula along with normalization of their relations, but the future requires much more diplomacy. To achieve so many simultaneous goals will require the design of a "road map" by skilled negotiators who will learn the lessons of diplomacy in Chapter 3 and apply them conscientiously to future negotiations between North Korea and the United States. There may be ups and downs, so both sides will have to learn to be patient rather than in a hurry. But following the logic of the Community Building Paradigm will assure success.

References

Bailey, Stephen K. (1992). *The Korean Armistice*. New York: St. Martin's Press.
Bercovitch, Jacob, and Scott Gartner (2006). "Is There Method in the Madness of Mediation? Some Lessons for Mediators from Quantitative Studies of Mediation," *International Interactions*, 32 (4): 329–354.
Bercovitch, Jacob, and Richard Jackson (1997). *International Conflict: A Chronological Encyclopedia of Conflicts and Their Management 1945–1995*. Washington, DC: Washington Quarterly.
Fehrs, Matthew (2016). "Letting Bygones Be Bygones: Rapprochement in US Foreign Policy," *Foreign Policy Analysis*, 12 (2): 128–148.
Ghosn, Faten (2010). "Getting to the Table and Getting to Yes: An Analysis of International Negotiations," *International Studies Quarterly*, 54 (4): 1055–1072.
Howard, Peter (2004). "Why Not Invade North Korea? Threats, Language Games, and U.S. Foreign Policy," *International Studies Quarterly*, 48 (4): 805–828.
Lasswell, Harold D. (1951). *The Policy Sciences*. Stanford, CA: Stanford University Press.
Snyder, Scott (1999). *Negotiating on the Edge: North Korean Negotiating Behavior*. Washington, DC: U.S. Institute of Peace Press.
Sun Key-Young (2006). *South Korean Engagement Policies and North Korea: Identities, Norms and the Sunshine Policy*. New York: Routledge.
Trumbore, Peter F. (1998). "Public Opinion as a Domestic Constraint in International Negotiations: Two-Level Games in the Anglo-Irish Peace Process," *International Studies Quarterly*, 42 (3): 545–565.
World Bank (2017). "The World Bank in Vietnam," *worldbank.org*, April 13. Accessed August 7, 2017.

EPILOGUE

North Korea and World War III

History often repeats itself. Based on the experience of World Wars I and II, the world was once close to World War III.

The person most responsible for World War I was Kaiser Wilhelm. He not only gave a "blank check" to Austria for reprisals against Serbia but also was the first to send troops into a major battle.

Communiqués sent between leaders in mid-1914 reveal that the Kaiser's motivation was revenge against disrespect. Messages became increasingly hostile to the point that the Kaiser felt compelled to protect his honor by attacking and defeating France before Russian troops were on his doorstep, even though he knew that the prospect for German aggression was bleak (Zinnes, North, Koch 1961).

At one point, Kaiser said, "If we are to be bled to death, at least England shall lose India" (quoted in Fischer 1967:121). In other words, he did not care whether Germany would suffer a catastrophic loss. What mattered was that his enemy would suffer, too.

Similarly, Kim Jong Un's father was once asked how North Korea would respond if the United States launched an attack. He answered, "If we lose, I will be sure to destroy the Earth. What good is the Earth without North

Korea?" (quoted in Ignatius 2017). Today, Pyongyang has an underground city just in case (Robinson 2017), while most of the rest of the world is unprepared for a nuclear holocaust.

During 2017, Kim Jong Un and Donald Trump duplicated the exchange of words that preceded World War I. Although Trump may not care that he is the most disrespectful president in American history, Kim does mind. For Koreans and other Asians, showing personal disrespect is not taken lightly. Kim interpreted *The Interview* as extreme disrespect and cyberattacked the studio that produced the film in 2014. But Trump's comments went light years beyond *The Interview*, but he was more flattering in 2018. Negative comments on Trump from North Korea during 2017 turned to positive in private communications during early 2018.

DPRK's foreign minister once indicated that a missile attack on the United States is "inevitable," given what he considered Trump's declaration of war (Demick 2017). If history repeated itself, Kim would have launched a thermonuclear attack at his enemies even though North Korea would be massively destroyed.

Meanwhile, there were fears that Kim is developing submarines to carry nuclear missiles (Hartmann 2017). Added to the longstanding program to develop biological and chemical weapons, the growing arsenal in North Korea was provoking Washington to consider a preemptive strike. And no continuing diplomacy for years involved Pyongyang with China, the United Nations, or the United States.

But once World War III began, other aggression might be in store. While Washington is preoccupied with North Korea, some 40,000 Russian troops are massed on the border of Ukraine, ready for deployment far beyond (Charlton 2016). China has long relied on North Korea as a buffer against hostile forces of the United States and might enter the war, as before, to prevent reunification of the Korean peninsula (Le Miere 2017). The Chinese navy might encircle Taiwan while the United States was preoccupied.

In short, a worst-case scenario was unfolding, with planetary consequences far beyond the "fire and fury" of Trump's irresponsible rhetoric (Baker and Choe 2017). The question then was how to de-escalate and promote bilateral or multilateral diplomacy to achieve peace and stability on the Korean peninsula.

All three ignored the possibility that North Korea merely wants to achieve a nuclear deterrent, similar to Britain, China, France, India, Israel, Pakistan, and the United States. That assurance was provided by North Korea on December 24, 2017 (Blanchard and Shin 2017). Talks between Kim and Trump became the only way to ascertain Pyongyang's true intentions (Kristian 2017).

Then discussion reverted to imposing sanctions. Although neither China nor Russia welcomed a nuclear North Korea. Trump's conduct on the international stage does not encourage compliance by other countries, (Horton 2018). The UN sanctions resolution of December 2017 also called for the resumption of Six-Party Talks, so American failure to return to negotiations would have been excuse for sanctions noncompliance. Besides, Moscow wants to weaken the United States, and now Moscow has the opportunity to observe Washington's increasing isolation in the world community. In light of Trump's disdain for multilateral alliances, Beijing and Moscow seem to enjoy filling in the power vacuum—and North Korea's need for oil (Faulconbridge, Saul, Nikolskaya 2017; Wen and Brunnstrom 2017).

Some observers believe that sanctions worked with Iran, so they would force North Korea to the negotiating table. But the difference is that the Iranian people elected a president who was eager to negotiate and to counterbalance hardliners in his government. No such civil society has even restrained the government in Pyongyang.

But what if sanctions worked? On November 29, 2017, the American UN ambassador proposed cutting off all oil shipments from China to North Korea, but the UN Security Council's sanctions of December 22, 2017, stopped short of that goal.

However, the last time oil sanctions were applied in a similar situation was in 1941, when the United States stopped all oil shipments to Japan. The direct result was the attack on Pearl Harbor, even though Tokyo suspected that the United States would ultimately prevail (Yergin 1991). Japanese Foreign Ministry officials were outside the offices of the American Secretary of State on December 7, 1941, ready to negotiate, but Japan's Cabinet was dominated by the military and would not wait for diplomacy to work.

That left the unpredictability of Donald Trump as yet another uncertainty. The proposal to shoot down a North Korean missile launch, if carried out, would definitely serve as a pretext for war, according to North Korean defector Thae Yong Ho (PBS 2017). And Pyongyang claimed the same right if an American warplane flies near North Korea.

Dramatic diplomacy by China, a major power without a megalomaniac in charge, might have worked. Because Europe may be affected, a multilateral conference in Geneva or Paris might serve to cool the situation. But the

United States would have to pay the cost if someone else fills the diplomacy vacuum created by Trump, who crucified any claim to American benevolent world leadership in his first UN address (Calamur 2017; Yarhi-Milo 2018:76).

Surely the American people, political parties, the corporate community, and the media would have been an overwhelming chorus of opposition to Trump's dangerous policies and rhetoric before it was too late. But they were engaged in wishful thinking about sanctions.

While the situation intensified, talk about the need for a preemptive American strike increased in Washington. And, as if to confirm that option, Senator Lindsay Graham in mid-December called for the evacuation of American civilians from South Korea (Rogan 2017).

Graham doubtless was aware that the United States is technically still at war with North Korea, since neither South Korea nor the United States signed the armistice agreement in 1953. Although Pyongyang repeatedly called for peace negotiations, no American president agreed to hold talks to end the war.

When 2018 began, no one in the United States government was in favor of war. War was also opposed by China, Russia, and both Koreas. Because war was not an option, the obvious conclusion was that peace is the option. North Korea has long sought a peace treaty with the United States, but Washington has consistently refused to negotiate on that basis—and even criticized South Korea for wanting to engage in talks with the North (Denyer 2018). While seeking a peace agreement, DPRK leaders have tried several ways to get Washington to the negotiating table, but in vain. Accordingly, the DPRK was left with the impression that peace would only come after there was a nuclear standoff between the two countries. Just as that day arrived, South Korean voters elected Moon Jae In, a president who proposed to reach out to the North. After Kim Jong Un expressed interest in participating in the Olympic Games in South Korea, the two leaders met. Kim then expressed interest in meeting Trump, and bilateral diplomacy between North Korea and the United States revived to the point of a summit meeting in Singapore during June 2018.

Many lessons were learned from the sequence of events since Donald Trump became president: (1) The precondition to the Singapore summit was achieved as the two leaders undertook a series of unilateral reciprocated measures of confidence building. (2) They established a warm personal relationship before and during the summit, the first step in any successful diplomacy. (3) The Singapore Declaration established a set of goals for future diplomatic interaction. In other words, they achieved the second step required in diplomacy – agenda setting.

(4) The immediate consequence was that the threat of World War III no longer haunts the world. (5) After the summit, more confidence-building measures were promised – shutdown of a North Korean missile test site in exchange for a cancellation of American-South Korean war games. (6) The events prove that Asian community-building diplomacy is preferable to Western deterrence- and contract-oriented diplomacy when the task is to deal with long-time adversaries. (7) Those who believed that North Korea would never give up nuclear weapons now must realize that Pyongyang never wanted them in the first place: They were developed to deter an aggressive foreign policy of the United States that has now changed. (8) The future depends upon whether lower-level negotiators will succeed in carrying out the comprehensive agenda set forth in Singapore. They have stumbled in the past, but now both leaders will be looking over their shoulders, hopefully insisting on progress.

The journey of American diplomacy with North Korea has been much more perilous than with Vietnam, so it would be unwise to imagine inevitable success down the road in dealing with Pyongyang. Both American and North Korean negotiators will be well served by reviewing the past diplomatic history between the two countries and showing more diligence and patience in the years ahead.

References

Baker, Peter, and Choe Sang-Hun (2017). "Trump Threatens 'Fire and Fury' Against North Korea If It Endangers U.S.," *New York Times*, August 8.

Blanchard, Ben, and Hyonhee Shin (2017). "North Korea Rejects New UN Sanctions, Calls Them an 'Act of War'," *reuters.com*, December 24.

Browne, Ryan, and Nicole Gaouette (2017). "Mattis Says North Korea Isn't Capable of Striking the US," *cnn.com*, December 16.

Calamur, Krishnadev (2017). "How the Rest of the World Heard Trump's UN Speech," *The Atlantic*, September 21. Accessed November 24, 2017.

Charlton, Corey (2016). "Fears of All-Out Conflict in Ukraine as Sabre-Rattling Vladimir Putin Places 40,000 Troops and Armoured Vehicles along the Border," *thesun.co.uk/news/1631749*, August 16. Accessed November 24, 2017.

Demick, Barbara (2017). "Can U.S. and North Korea Get Back to Negotiations?," *Los Angeles Times*, August 11.

Denyer, Simon (2018). "South Korea Welcomes North's Offer of Talks," *Washington Post*, January 2.

Faulconbridge, Guy, Jonathan Saul, and Polina Nikoskaya (2017). "Russian Tankers Fueled North Korea Via Transfers at Sea: Sources," *reuters.com*, December 28.

Fischer, Fritz (1967). *Germany's Aims in the First World War*. New York: Norton.
Hartmann, Margaret (2017). "North Korea May Also Be Developing Submarine Missiles and Biological Weapons," *intelligencer.com*, December 11.
Horton, Chris (2018). "Taiwan Citizens Accused of Violating U.N. Sanctions on North Korea," *New York Times*, January 31.
Ignatius, David (2017). "In Dealing with North Korea, Trump Needs Allies—Not Bombast," *Washington Post*, August 10.
Kristian, Bonnie (2017). "In North Korea, It's a Question of Intent," *Los Angeles Times*, December 22.
Le Miere, Jason (2017). "China Would Join Forces with North Korea If U.S. Launches Pre-Emptive Strike," *Newsweek*, August 11.
Public Broadcasting System (2017). "North Korean Defector Says Even a Limited Attack by U.S. Would Trigger All-Out War," *pbs.com*, November 3.
Robinson, Julian (2017). "Is This Why Kim Is So 'Unafraid'? North Korea Boasts the World's Deepest Underground Metro System, Meaning Pyongyang Residents Can Hide 360ft Underground If Nuclear War Breaks Out," *dailymail.com*, August 11.
Rogan, Tom (2017). "Lindsay Graham Is Right: It's Time to Evacuate US Dependents from South Korea," *Washington Examiner*, December 4.
Wen, Philip, and David Brunnstrom (2017). "After Trump Criticism, China Denies Selling Oil Illicitly to North Korea," *reuters.com*, November 29.
Yarhi-Milo, Keren (2018). "After Credibility: American Foreign Policy in the Trump Era," *Foreign Policy*, 97 (1): 68–77.
Yergin, Daniel (1991). "Blood and Oil: Why Japan Attacked Pearl," *Washington Post*, December 1. Accessed November 24, 2017.
Zinnes, Dina A., Robert C. North, and Howard E. Koch, Jr. (1961). "Capability, Threat, and the Outbreak of War." In *International Politics and Foreign Policy*, ed. James N. Rosenau, pp. 469–482. New York: Free Press.

AFTERWORD

Johan Galtung

What is U.S. diplomacy? After U.S. bombing killed 3.5 million in Korea from 1950 to 1953, and the U.S. Army killed 3 million in Vietnam from 1961 (under Kennedy) to 30 April 1975 (under Ford). Softer?

This very rich, well-researched book by Michael Haas—a senior, major U.S. political scientist—gives detailed "softer" empirical, factual answers in Part II. Indeed, this book is highly recommended.

However, I want to explore the "deep culture" implications of U.S. foreign policy, compared with "U.S. diplomacy."

The self-image of the United States is as successor to Israel as most favored nation—by God, with Chosen People and Promised Land (CPPL). Such a vision started in 1620—on the *Mayflower*. In contrast, the "existence of the 'Jewish State'" over the past seventy years demonstrates that Israel does not enjoy CPPL status; that existed only under King David and the kings who followed Solomon.

In other words, during 1620 *the position of CPPL was empty*. Puritan Pilgrims from East Anglia via Leiden in Holland applied for that status. London, with no chosen people but command of the promise land, was beaten in a War of Independence from 1775–1812 for Promised Land for Chosen People, ushering in 141 years of wars seeking "unconditional surrender." Up to then, the USA appeared to be invincible.

The Korean War 1950–1953, even with a Uniting for Peace UN mandate, ended not with victory but ceasefire, armistice, a demilitarized zone, having been strongly resisted by North Korea and China. The war in Vietnam, from 1961 until April 30, 1975, ended with the U.S. Army withdrawing unconditionally.

Four stages can be recognized in this very recent history:

- French then Japanese colonization of Vietnam; Japanization of Korea.
- Defeat of Japan; Vietnam given back to France; Korea divided by the USSR and USA.
- Nationalisms, both against France and USSR–USA, for independence.
- USA belligerence against national independence, keeping South Korea, but losing Vietnam.

The role of "USA Diplomacy"? To justify U.S. aggression; and, if war does not work, to justify "softer approaches," such as negotiation.

The role of "USA Democracy"? A personal story is illustrative:

The story involves Dennis Kucinich, Democratic member of the House of Representatives from Ohio before he was gerrymandered away—another aspect of U.S. democracy, fair and free elections in practice. One day he organized a meeting in his office suite in the building across the street from Congress. At that meeting, he asked me to tell some representatives about my encounter with Taliban leaders in Afghanistan. For the Taliban, the problem was the 1893 Durand Line between the British Empire—now Pakistan—and Afghanistan. The line cut in two the lands of the biggest nation without a state—the Pashtuns. As a result, Pashtuns and Taliban became almost synonymous.

Solution: eliminate that line, create a *Central Asian Community*, border-free, with Afghanistan, Pakistan, the other "stans," Iran, and Kashmir. All the people would be in Afghanistan, and Afghanistan would be in them.

A Congressional Representative at Kucinich's meeting then said, "Taliban may think like that. But I am an elected representative in U.S. democracy. The people elected me for this—he made the V sign—then we will tell them what the solution is."

Today, a decade later, the USA is still fighting, with North Atlantic Treaty Organization (NATO) allies, for a victory and solution in Afghanistan that they will never obtain, because:

- Afghanistan is 98 percent Muslim, whereas the USA is national evangelist.
- Afghans can draw upon the solidarity of 1,650 million Muslims.

- The USA has deep problems, even with NATO allies.
- The time horizon of Afghans is unlimited, while the U.S. plans only for an administration or two.
- There are strong Muslim groups in the USA and allies, not vice versa.
- Muslims know the West, the languages, cultures, not vice versa.
- Afghans are today up against an "unleveled" U.S. president.

An unequal fight may tempt some in the USA to use nukes against a very invulnerable country, leading to revenge toward vulnerable USA. The outcome will be more isolation, decline, and the fall of the U.S. Republic.

That process has already started, as witnessed by the many major conferences to which the USA is no longer invited. The ball is now in other courts—in Russia, India, China and for the other two BRICS (Brazil and South Africa) in general.

Historically, "U.S. Diplomacy" seems to go through four stages:

- Tell other states what to do; if they comply, that is it.
- If they do not comply, attack them as anti-American enemies;
- If the U.S. wins, see to it that they comply and reward the compliers.
- If the U.S. does not win, try "softer approaches," such as negotiation, diplomacy.

What will happen if U.S. thinking about North Korea and Vietnam is at the same level as for Afghanistan? CIA? ("Central" no doubt, and "Agency," but how about the "Intelligence"?) The USA withdrew, badly wounded, from Vietnam, and is now heading for the same in Afghanistan.

North Korea: There seems to be a stalemate, with about eight million persons in and around Seoul being held as hostages to the North Korean artillery should there be a U.S. attack. North Korea will not launch a first strike, but they want to show the USA, Japan, and the World that they are equal to USA in offensive capability with an invulnerability of force and value—people— unmatched in human history.

Mantra: "1952" NEVER AGAIN!

Peace is around the corner if U.S. diplomacy were able to think–speak– act peace. Take North Korea at its word, ask them for the details of converting an armistice to a peace treaty, of normalizing diplomatic relations with Seoul–Tokyo–Washington, of a UN-inspected nuclear-free Korean Peninsula. And then: Negotiate. But much "USA Diplomacy" is used to oppose such a scenario because the USA really wants to control South Korea.

Vietnam: The U.S. defeat was total as opposed to Korea. There will be no war in the foreseeable future in spite of theories about how that unwinnable war could have been won. There was some diplomatic basis for the imposed division between North and South Vietnam, but how Vietnam overcame division should teach the USA a lesson about a divided North–South. Today, Vietnam has improved its *karma* with the USA. If the USA would learn to improve its *karma* with the world, peace would be around the corner.

Conclusion: The general problem is the U.S. deep culture as a Chosen People with a Promised *World*. The solution is for the USA to become *normal*.

INDEX

A

Abkhazia, 1
Acquired Immunodeficiency Deficiency Syndrome (AIDS), 38
Adzharskaya, 1
affection, 129
Afghanistan, 140–141. See also Taliban
agenda setting, 14, 68, 93, 100, 136–137
Agent Orange, 36
Agreed Framework between North Korea and the United States (1994), xii, 70–74, 76–77, 80–81, 108–109, 114
aid, bilateral, 37, 41
aid, economic, xvii, 23–26, 34, 36–38, 40–41, 45, 50–52, 62–63, 73, 77, 98, 111
aid, energy, 70, 83–84
aid, food, xiii, 63, 73, 85, 87, 110, 129
aid, humanitarian, xiii, xvii, 23–24, 34, 36–37, 42, 44, 62, 74, 81, 83–84, 109, 110

aid, military, 7, 22, 29, 50, 52, 62, 65, 68, 82
aid, multilateral, 37, 43
aid, private, 25–26, 42
aid, reconstruction. See aid, economic
aid embargo. See embargo, aid
Air France, 35
Air Vietnam, 35
Albright, Madeleine, 75–76
alliances, 8, 38, 46, 107, 113, 122, 135
allies, xv, 8, 11–12, 22, 24, 28–30, 45, 59, 68, 91, 97, 122, 124, 140–41
Allison, Graham, 93
ambassadors, xi, xv, xxi, 4, 41, 43, 77, 88, 95, 97, 127, 131, 135
Amerasians, 23, 30, 32–33, 50
American Telephone & Telegraph Company (AT&T), 42
armed forces, 5–6, 21, 23, 26, 28–30, 33, 39, 60, 64, 93, 113, 127, 139–140
armistice, xii, 60–62, 64–67, 83, 86–87, 90, 107, 113, 127, 129, 136, 140–141
arms embargo, 40, 45, 52

arms race, 90
arms sales, 7, 45, 69, 72, 76, 82, 108
artificial limbs, 36
Artsakh, 1
Asia, Central, 140
Asia, Northeast, 56, 122
Asia, Southeast, 25–26, 29, 32, 54
Asian Development Bank, 38, 43, 52, 63
Association for Asian Studies, 35
Association of South-East Asian Nations (ASEAN), 32, 80
"asymmetric capabilities" military exercises, 64
atomic bomb, 6, 89, 93, 117–118
atomic energy, 80
Australia, 24, 29, 30, 40, 62
Australian television, 27
Austria, 133
authoritarian rule, 125
authority, 14, 34, 42

B

back-channel negotiations, 5, 19, 50, 69, 90–91, 110–111, 117
Baker, James, III, 34, 41
balance of power, 70
balance of threats, 70
balloons, 24
bank account freeze, 6, 38, 45, 52, 81, 83, 109
Bank of America, 38
bargaining, 3, 14, 26, 89, 90, 92, 96, 99, 121–122, 129–130. See also negotiations
bargaining chips, xiii, 4, 62, 70, 82, 110
basic human needs, 42
Batista, Fulgencio, 5
battlefields, 19, 23–24
Belgium, 40, 62
Bergman, Michael, xiii
biological weapons, xvi, 134
birth defects, 36
Bitcoins, 91
"black box," 11, 14, 130

black market, 39
blackmail, 98, 118
"blank check," 133
body count, 24–25, 62
Bolton, John, 77, 98
Bosworth, Steven, 85, 87
boycotts, 5, 67, 88, 97, 115
"brainwashing," 62
Brazil, 141
breakdowns, 20
breast milk, 36
bribery. See blackmail
BRICS, 141
bridge loans, 42
Britain, 21, 30, 32, 41, 91, 134, 139–140
British soldiers fighting in Korea, 62
Brunei, 32
Brzezinski, Zbigniew, 28–29, 46, 62–63
building socialism, 39
bureaucracies, 31
Bush, George H. W., xx, 27, 30, 36–37, 43, 124
Bush, George W., xii, 45, 62, 76–79, 109, 122
businesses, xiii, xii, 3–6, 13, 40, 42, 51, 61, 67, 72, 89, 93, 112, 124

C

Cambodia, 54
Cambodia, cantonments, 42
Cambodia, elections, 30, 40, 43
Cambodia, ethnic Vietnamese, 27–28
Cambodia, independence, 8
Cambodia, Khmer Rouge, xix, 6, 23, 25, 27–30
Cambodia, parliament, 30, 43
Cambodia, peace agreements, 6, 21, 30, 40–43, 124
Cambodia, relations with Australia, 30, 41
Cambodia, relations with Britain, 41
Cambodia, relations with China, 27–28
Cambodia, relations with France, 41

Cambodia, relations with Italy, 41
Cambodia, relations with Laos, 22
Cambodia, relations with the Soviet Union, 46
Cambodia, relations with Thailand, 28–29
Cambodia, relations with the United States, xix–xx, 6, 8, 22, 26, 28–30, 36, 41, 50–51, 122, 124, 127
Cambodia, relations with Vietnam, 22, 25–30, 38, 42, 46, 50, 52–53, 122, 124–125, 127, 129–130
Cambodia, tourism, 36
Cambodia, transitional quadripartite government proposal, 29
Cambodia. See also Kampuchea; UN Transitional Authority for Cambodia
Canada, 22, 24, 62
Carter, Jimmy, 25, 28–29, 62, 65, 70, 72, 86, 100, 107, 114, 124, 130
Castro, Fidel, xii, 5
ceasefire, 22, 42, 60, 140
child deaths in wartime, 24
China, 54, 56
China, Bank of China, 83
China, civil war, 4
China, economy, 8, 39, 45, 63, 86, 92–93, 95, 112, 122
China, diplomacy, 4–5, 21, 77, 78–84, 88, 100, 127, 135, 135
China, military, xiv, 4, 9, 45, 60, 62, 93, 121–123, 134, 140–141
China, radio broadcasts, 30
China, relations with Cambodia, 27–28
China, relations with North Korea, 8, 60, 65–66, 68, 77–92, 94–95, 98, 111–112, 122, 134–135
China, relations with Russia, 122
China, relations with South Korea, 5, 60, 66, 86, 88, 90
China, relations with the Soviet Union, 28
China, relations with the United States, 8, 19, 25, 28, 45–46, 60, 65, 78–87, 89–93, 95, 111–112, 122, 131, 134

China, relations with Vietnam, 8, 19, 28–30, 32, 46, 122
China, tourism, 93
China, Yalu River, 73
China. See also Republic of China; South China Sea
Chinese People's Volunteers, 60
"Chosen People," 139, 142
Christians, 98
Christopher, Warren, 44
civil society, 13, 20, 126, 130, 135
civil unrest, 8
civil wars, 5, 7–8, 12, 22, 24
civilian war casualties, 37, 64
civilian evacuation, 136
civilian war casualties, 37, 64
Clapper, James, 88
Clinton, Bill, xi, xii, 40, 43, 45–46, 62, 68, 72–76, 86, 124, 127, 130
Cohen, William, 75
Cold War, 5, 7–8, 34, 46, 61–62, 66, 68–69, 122, 125
Colombia, 62
colonial rule, 5, 21
"common language," 14, 67
Communist countries, 4, 7, 34, 39, 43, 46, 62
Community Building Paradigm, xx, 11, 14, 15, 126–139
concessions, 4, 11–12, 14–15, 29, 38, 46, 53, 79–80, 84, 90, 122–130
condition, necessary, 14
condition, sufficient, 14
condoms, 38
confidence-building measures, xi, 14–15, 20, 25–26, 96, 98–100, 122, 127, 130–131, 136–137
conservatism, 7
consortiums, 40, 71
consulates, 3, 44
Coolidge, Calvin, 4, 7, 8
Cooperman, Edward, 35
Costa Rica, 4, 7
coups d'état, 7
Cranston, Alan, xx

credit guarantees, 45
Cuba, 5, 8, 19, 131
cultural perspectives, 15, 130
cyberattacks, 87, 90, 115, 132
cyberwar, 9, 111
Czech Republic, 61, 114
Czechoslovakia, 40, 61

D

death threats, 35
de-escalation, xx, 67, 93, 96–99, 134
demilitarization, 67
demilitarized zones, 21, 60–61, 140
demobilization of troops, 42–43
democracy, 13, 30, 66, 125–126, 130, 140
Democratic Front for the Reunification of the Fatherland, 59
Democratic People's Republic of Korea. See North Korea
Democratic Republic of Kampuchea. See Kampuchea
Democratic Republic of Vietnam. See North Vietnam
democratization, 125
denuclearization, xii, xvi, 67, 69, 77–81, 84, 86–90, 93–94, 96–98, 100, 107, 109–111, 114–118
deterrence, 12, 28, 66, 69–70, 86, 89–90, 94, 100, 118, 122–123, 125, 129, 134, 137
Deterrence Paradigm, xx, 11–12, 66, 100, 121–123, 126, 129
dictatorship, 13
dioxin, 36
diplomacy, contract-oriented, 137
diplomacy, creative, xvi, 101
diplomacy, failure of, xi, xix, 20, 68, 124–125
diplomacy international, 1, 134
diplomacy, opposition to, 93, 112
diplomacy, "ping-pong," 19
diplomacy, private, xv
diplomacy, quest for, xv, xvi–xvii, xx, 14, 25, 29–30, 41, 68–70, 75, 78, 87–88, 96–97, 100–1, 120

diplomacy, secret, 6. See also back-channel negotiations
diplomacy, successful, xi–xii, 14, 124, 127, 130, 132
diplomacy, value of, xii–xv, xvii, 1, 3, 9, 15, 23–24, 30, 35, 44, 46, 52, 69, 71, 78, 80, 98–99, 127–28, 131, 136–37, 141
diplomatic normalization, xii, 1, 3–9, 11, 19, 21, 23–24, 30, 39, 43–46, 52, 65, 78, 80, 83, 98, 121, 131, 141
diplomatic process, 14–15, 20
diplomatic suspension, 4–6, 8, 23, 95, 113
diplomats, exchange of, 3, 5, 43–44, 66
diplomats, xx, 3, 6, 25, 41, 51, 86, 89, 91, 95, 97, 107, 127, 130–131
disabled persons, 24, 36
distrust, 20, 128
Dominican Republic, 4, 7
double-crossing, xx, 20
dual citizenship, 44
dual exchange rate, 39
Dunford, Joseph, 92
Durand Line, 140

E

economic agreements, 39, 80, 89, 109
economic aid. See aid, economics
economic assets, 45
economic autonomy, 125
economic change, 13, 124–25, 129–30
economic development, xvii, 86
economic dissatisfaction, 39
economic dominance, 6
dependence, economic, 38
economic incentives, 14, 98
economic inputs, 34, 46, 79, 94, 124
economic interests, 6, 38–40
economic migrants, 30, 32
economic normalization. See normalization, economic
economic pain, 32, 39, 85, 125
economic power, 112, 63, 86, 125

economic reconstruction, 25
economic reforms, 38, 63, 76, 87
economic retaliation, 90
economic sanctions. See sanctions, economic
economic shortfalls, 35, 94
economic transactions. See trade; embargo, trade
economic weakness, 29, 125
economy, capitalist, 13, 38
economy, planned, 13, 124
Eisenhower, Dwight, 22
elections, xiii, 6, 8–9, 22, 30, 36, 40, 43, 50, 59–60, 65, 67, 75–76, 85, 96, 127, 140
Ellsberg, Daniel, xx
embargo, arms, 40, 45, 52
embargo, economic. See sanctions, economic
embargo, personal, 89
embargo, trade. See sanctions, economic
embassies, xiv, 4–6, 8, 23, 26–27, 30, 33, 35, 44–45
enemies, xii, xvii, 1, 5–6, 8, 15, 25, 37, 38, 46, 62, 121, 127, 133–134, 141
England. See Britain
enlightenment, 129
equidistance policy, 28
escalation, xx, 3, 85, 90–97, 134
Ethiopia, 62
Europe, 7, 43, 135
Europe, Eastern, 5, 35, 38, 62
Europe, Western, 7, 35, 52
European banks, 63
European businesses, 126
evangelism, 140
Evans, Gareth, 30
exchange, quid pro quo, xiii, xiv, xvi, 6, 21, 69, 70–72, 74, 77, 79–84, 95, 98–100, 136–37
exchange programs, 36, 129
exchange rates, 39, 69, 72
exchanges, communication, 66, 77, 97, 134
exchanges, military, 23, 61, 88
"expanded capabilities" military exercises, 64

F

Feltman, Jeffrey, 95–96
film industry, 24, 88, 117, 134
"fire and fury" threat (2017), 134
First National City Bank, 38
Ford, Gerald, 24, 124, 139
foreign exchange, 35, 39–40, 69, 72
foreign policy analysis, xx, 11–15, 121–32
France, 5, 6, 29–30, 40–42, 51, 62, 133–134, 136–37, 140
France, military, 5, 21–22, 62, 133–134
France, relations with Japan, 21
France, relations with the United States, 5, 21, 51
France, relations with Vietnam, 21–22, 29, 40–42, 51, 140
"fremenies," 12, 15
friendly gestures, 15
friendly relations, xx, 4, 8, 20–21, 46, 61
frozen assets. See bank account freeze

G

Galtung, Johan, xxi, 138–42
Geneva Accords, 21, 129
Geneva conferences, 21, 31–32, 60
Geneva Conventions, xiii
genocide, 28, 94
Genocide by Proxy: Cambodian Pawn on a Superpower Chessboard, xx
Georgia, 9
Germany, 7–8, 133
Germany, relations with Russia, 133
goods, consumer, 35, 39, 65
goods, private, 13, 125
goods, public, 13–14, 123, 128
goods, strategic, 38
Gorbachëv, Mikhail, 35
Gore, Al, 75
Graham, Lindsay, 136
Gregg, Donald, 131
guerrilla warfare, 22

H

Haïti, 4, 7
Hall, James, 43
Harding, Warren, 7
hegemony, 4
Hill, Christopher, 80, 82, 84
Hồ Chí Minh, 5, 21–22
Holland. See Netherlands
Hollywood films. See films
Honda Motor Company, 40, 51
Honduras, 4, 8
Hongkong, British, 32, 63
hostages, xiii, xiv, 6, 65, 88, 91, 117–118, 128, 141
hostility, xii–xiii, xx, 8–9, 14, 34, 39, 61, 64, 67, 77, 91, 93, 98, 107, 133–134
How to Sweet-Talk a Shark: Strategies and Stories from a Master Negotiator, xii
Howard, Peter, 70
human rights, xvi, 44–45, 51, 80, 82, 90, 98, 110
Human Rights Dialog between the United States and Vietnam, 45
"human waves," 60
humanitarian aid. See aid, humanitarian
humanitarian intervention, 28–29
humanitarian issues, xiv, 23, 26, 30–34, 41, 46, 93
"Hungarian reforms," 39, 125
Hunziker, Evan, xii, 73

I

immigrants, xii, 31–33, 35, 50, 124
independence, 4–5, 8, 21, 137–138
India, 22, 40, 60, 133–134, 141
Indochina, 21, 24, 27, 60. See also Cambodia; Laos; Vietnam
Indonesia, 31–32
inflation, 39
instability, domestic, 4
integration, 14
Interest Sections, 4, 26

interference in internal affairs, 4, 37. See also noninterference in internal affairs
International Atomic Energy Agency (IAEA), 68–69, 70–71, 76–77, 82–87, 108, 113–117
International Atomic Energy Agency safeguards agreement, 68, 76
International Conference on Indo-Chinese Refugees, 31–32
International consortium, 71
International Control Commission, 22
International Criminal Court, 88
international law, xiii, 28
International Monetary Fund (IMF), 38, 43, 63
International Olympic Committee, 67
International Peace Research Association, xxi
international public opinion, 41
international relations, normal, 3
international students, 36
international system, 1, 130, 135
Internet age, 75
intervention, military, 7–9, 28
interviewing, xix–xx, 19, 27, 31–33, 99
investment, xvii, 23, 38–40, 43–44, 63, 74, 80
investment guarantees, 39
Iran, xv, 6, 9, 69, 72, 74–76, 89, 91, 112–113, 134, 138
Israel, 134
Italy, 41, 67

J

Japan, economy, 39, 40, 43, 52, 63
Japan, military, 5, 21, 95, 135, 140
Japan, North Korean residents, 63
Japan, Okinawa, 95
Japan, postwar occupation, 60
Japan, relations with France, 21
Japan, relations with North Korea, xiv, 63, 66, 72–73, 77–79, 84, 87–88, 91–92, 94–95, 98, 117–118, 141

Japan, relations with North Vietnam, 5, 21
Japan, relations with Russia, 93
Japan, relations with South Korea, 72, 88, 93, 95
Japan, relations with the United States, 5, 43, 52, 60, 88, 135
Japan, relations with Vietnam, 21, 39, 40, 43, 52, 140
Japanese in North Korea, 78, 91, 115
Johnson, Lyndon, 22
Joint Statement (1993), 69, 71
Joint Statement (2005), 80–83, 85
Journal of Peace Research, xxi

K

Kaiser Wilhelm II, 133
Kalugin, Oleg, 27
Kampuchea, Democratic Republic of, 6. See also Cambodia
Kampuchea, People's Republic of, 28. See also Cambodia
Kang, David, 70
karma, 142
Kashmir, 140
Kazakhstan, 27
Kelly, James, 78
Kennedy, John F., 139
Khmer Empire, 23
Khmer Krom, 23
Khmer Rouge. See Cambodia
Kim Dae Jung, 67, 74, 122
Kim Il Sung, xii, 59, 64, 70, 72
Kim Jong Il, xii–xiii, 75–76, 79, 87, 133
Kim Jong Nam, 91, 95
Kim Jong Un, xiv–xvii, xx, 68, 87–90, 93–98, 100, 125, 130–131, 134–136
Kim Kye Gwan, xii
King David, 139
King Solomon, 139
Koizumi, Junichirō, 77
Korea, 38th parallel, 59–60, 62
Korea, armistice violations, 60, 65–66
Korea, colony of Japan, 59, 140

Korea, demilitarized zone (DMZ), 60–61, 64–65, 90, 113, 117, 140
Korea, division of, 60
Korea, Joint Declaration on Denuclearization (1991), 69, 71
Korea, Military Armistice Commission (MAC), 60, 66, 87
Korea, Neutral Nations Supervisory Commission (NNSC), 60–61, 64, 87, 113–114
Korea, Panmunjom, 60, 62, 66, 97, 116
Korea, reunification plans, 59, 61, 65, 134
Korea, Yeonpeong, 66
Korea. See also North Korea; South Korea
Korean Energy Development Organization (KEDO), 71–72, 74
Korean Reunification: Alternative Pathways, xix
Korean War, xiii, 5, 98, 140
Korean War Armistice Agreement, 60
Kosovo, 1
Kucinich, Dennis, 140

L

land mines, 36, 90
Laos, 21–22, 32, 54
Laos, relations with North Vietnam, 22
Lasswell, Harold, 128
latex gloves, 38
Latin America, 6–7, 9
leaders, business, xii
leaders, "dove," 12, 122–24, 129
leaders, "hawk," 12–13, 122–24, 129
leaders, long-time, 11
leaders, needs of, 12, 100
leaders, new, 11, 123–24, 129
leaders, political, xvi, xx, 12–13, 15, 61, 64–65, 67, 84–85, 89–90, 93, 96, 98, 100–101, 110–112, 115, 117–118, 125, 127, 129–130, 133, 136–137, 140
leadership, domestic, 11, 46, 123–24, 126, 129, 131
leadership, world, 135–136

Lee Myung Bak, 67
leftism, 6–7
Liaison Offices, 4, 42–44
Libya, 80–81, 98, 113, 118
loan arrears, 38, 40, 42, 43
rockets, 73, 75, 87–88, 91, 95, 116–117
Lon Nol, 27
Lord, Winston, 43

M

MacArthur, Douglas, 60
Macau, Banco Delta Asia, 81
major powers, 1, 21, 59, 78, 135
Malaysia, 31, 32
Maldives, 4
Marxism, 40, 62
Mass Society Paradigm, 11, 13, 126, 130
"mass society," 13
Mattis, James "Mad Dog," 92–93
Mayflower, 137
McCain, John, 26–27, 46, 126
McGovern, George, 28
media, ci, 20, 78, 136
mediation, xxi, 15, 78–79, 81, 100, 127
medical aid, 37, 129
México, 4, 7, 8
missile capabilities, xv, 64, 66, 68–69, 74–75, 78, 81–82, 87–91, 98, 108, 111–112, 114–116, 118, 125, 134–135
missile policies, 72–76, 78–85
missile proliferation, 72–76
missile sales, 68–69, 73–75, 77, 110, 114–118, 128–129
Missile Technology Control Regime, 72–73
missile tests, 68, 73, 74–95, 97, 106, 108, 112–116, 126–127
Mobil Oil Company, 40
mobilization, troops, 28. See also demobilization
Moon Jae In, 97, 100, 136

Moscow Conference (1945), 59
most-favored-nation trade status, 43, 45
motorbikes, 39, 40
Mrazek, Robert, 33
Muslims, 140, 141
mutual defense agreements, 60, 67, 93
mutual distrust, 20, 64
mutual threats, 12
mutual trust, xiv, xvii, 14, 96, 98

N

nationalism, 140
nationalization, 5
natural rubber, 38
needs assessments, 36
negotiation "road maps," 24, 40–44, 51, 53, 70–76, 100–101, 132
negotiations, xii, xv–xvii, xx, 1, 3, 6, 11, 14–15, 19–26, 33–34, 41, 44, 46, 50–53, 60–61, 64–65, 68, 70–71, 76–85, 88–97, 99–101, 107–19, 121–23, 125, 129–32, 135–36, 140–41. See also bargaining
negotiators, xi–xii, xiv–xv, xvii, 14, 26, 69, 80, 83, 85, 87–88, 91, 101, 127, 130, 132, 137
Netherlands, 40, 62
neutrality in wartime, 7, 22, 93
New Zealand, 24
Newcomb, Richard, 45
Nguyễn Cơ Thạch, 25–26, 34, 41, 127, 130–131
Nguyễn Mẫn Cam, 41
Nguyễn Xuân Oánh, 39
Nicaragua, 6–7, 8
Nixon, Richard, 22–23, 65, 123
Nobel Peace Prize, xix, xxi, 67
nonaggression agreement, 79, 80, 87, 107, 109, 116
nongovernmental organizations, 13, 26, 35–40, 42, 46, 62–63, 126, 129–130, 135

INDEX

noninterference in internal affairs, 69, 107. See also interference in internal affairs
nonrecognition, diplomatic, 1, 3–9, 11–12, 131
normalization, complete, xi, xix–xx, 1–3, 5–7, 9, 23
normalization, diplomatic. See diplomatic normalization
normalization, economic, 24–45, 52, 69, 71, 75, 78
normalization, theories of, 11–15, 121–32
North American Free Trade Association (NAFTA), 8
North Atlantic Treaty Organization (NATO), 140–141
North Korea, 56, 59
North Korea, agreement violations, 65, 68–69, 72–74, 76–77, 79, 81–82, 84–87, 99, 113–117
North Korea, armed infiltration of South Korea, 64, 113
North Korea, arrests of Americans, xii, xiii–xiv, 65, 88, 91, 114, 116–117, 128, 141
North Korea, back-channel talks, 69, 90–91, 110–111, 117
North Korea, banking, 63, 73, 82–83
North Korea, bombing of aircraft, xii, 66, 71, 113
North Korea, *chuch'e* ideology, 63
North Korea, coastline, 64
North Korea, conventional armed forces, 5, 60, 64–65, 70, 113
North Korea, counterfeiting, 81
North Korea, deterrent force, 66, 70, 86, 89–90, 94, 100, 118, 122–123, 125, 129, 134
North Korea, diplomatic relations, 5, 59, 65–66, 95, 107
North Korea, economic aid received, 63, 77
North Korea, economy, xvii, 63, 69, 72–73, 75, 79–82, 86, 91–92, 96, 129, 134–35
North Korea, electricity generation, 65, 68, 69, 70–71, 76–78, 80, 109

North Korea, famine, 63
North Korea, foreign exchange, 69, 72, 76
North Korea, foreign investment, xvii, 63, 74, 80
North Korea, harbors, 72
North Korea, heavy fuel oil shipments, 71–72, 77, 79–80, 82–83, 85, 87, 95–96, 109–110, 135
North Korea, Korean Central News Agency, 73
North Korea, Korean People's Army, 60, 64
North Korea, missile tests, 68–69, 73, 80–81, 86–91, 93–95, 99, 114–118, 128–129
North Korea, moratorium on missile tests, 74–77, 80–81, 87, 97, 115, 117–118
North Korea, negotiation concessions with the United States, 62, 65, 72–75, 79–88, 92, 95–100, 113–118
North Korea, negotiation deviousness with the United States, 60, 62, 64–66, 68–72, 77–81, 83–95, 98–99, 113–118, 135
North Korea, "no first use" pledge, 81, 116
North Korea, nuclear tests, xiii, 79, 81, 86–90, 93, 95–96, 99, 110, 115–118, 128–129
North Korea, Olympic Games, 66–67, 96–97, 113, 136
North Korea, Operation Glory, 62
North Korea, peace treaty proposals, 65, 68, 75, 80, 83–84, 87–89, 94, 98, 100, 113, 117–118, 122, 127, 136, 141
North Korea, propaganda, xiii
North Korea, Pyongyang, 57, 63, 66, 110, 116, 134
North Korea, rationality in foreign policy, 66, 121–123, 126–128
North Korea, relatives of Koreans in Japan, 62
North Korea, relatives of Koreans in South Korea, 67
North Korea, relations with China, 8, 60, 65–66, 68, 77–92, 94–95, 98, 111–112, 122, 134–135

North Korea, relations with Japan, xiv, 63, 66, 72–73, 77–79, 84, 87–88, 91–92, 94–95, 98, 117–118, 141
North Korea, relations with Russia and the Soviet Union, 1, 59–62, 65–66, 68, 78–79, 83–86, 88, 91–92, 94–95, 97, 122–123, 135–136
North Korea, relations with South Korea, xiv, 59–69, 72–74, 78–79, 83–84, 86–89, 91–92, 94, 96–98, 100, 113, 116, 118, 122, 136–137, 141
North Korea, relations with the United States, xii, xiv–xvi, xix, 4–6, 19–20, 59–101, 107–118, 122–137
North Korea, relatives in Japan, 63, 66
North Korea, releases of captured Americans, xii–xiii, xiv, 65–66, 73, 88, 91, 97, 100, 115, 117–118
North Korea, remittances received from Japan, 63
North Korea, requests for compensation, 72–73, 75, 79
North Korea, sanctions, xiii, xv, 63, 65, 69, 73–96, 98, 108–112, 125, 130, 135–136
North Korea, satellite launches, 63, 73, 75, 85–87, 90, 110, 114, 116–117, 128
North Korea–South Korea Joint Declaration on Denuclearization, 67, 69, 79, 114
North Korea, submarines, 73, 134
North Korea, symphony orchestra, 97
North Korea, tourism/travel, 63, 67, 73, 113, 124, 129
North Korea, trade, xv, 62–63, 65, 69, 72–74, 76, 80–81, 86, 92–93, 107, 112. See also North Korea, sanctions
North Korea, travel, 73, 99, 111, 127
North Korea, underground city, 134
North Korea, unpaid loans, 63
North Korea, Yalu River, 73
North Korea, Yongbyon, 65, 70–71, 81–84, 88

North Korea–United States Agreed Framework (1994), xii, 70–74, 76–77, 80–81, 108–109, 114
North Korea–United States Joint Statement (1993), 69, 71
North Korea-United States Joint Statement (2005), 80–83, 85
North Korea–United States Leap Year Day Agreement (2012), 87
North Vietnam, agreement violations, 23–24, 52
North Vietnam, economy, 22–23, 36, 38–39, 126
North Vietnam, People's Army of Vietnam, 6, 23, 40, 46. See also Vietnam, People's Army of
North Vietnam, relations with Cambodia, 6, 22
North Vietnam, relations with Franc, 5, 21, 140
North Vietnam, relations with Japan, 21
North Vietnam, relations with Laos, 22
North Vietnam, relations with South Vietnam, 22–23
North Vietnam, relations with the United States, xix, xx, 5–6, 19, 21–23, 38–39, 50, 123, 126, 131
nuclear centrifuges, 74
Nuclear Non-Proliferation Treaty (NPT), 68–71, 77, 79–80, 113–116
nuclear power, peaceful uses of, 78–80, 82, 109
nuclear power plants, 6, 45, 65, 68, 76–78, 83–84
nuclear submarines, 89
nuclear tests, xiii, replace with 79, 81, 86–90, 93, 95–96, 99, 110, 115–118, 128–129
nuclear reactors, 69–70–77, 78, 81, 114, 116–117
nuclear warheads, 89, 92
nuclear weapons, xii, xiv–xvi, xix, xx, 6, 20, 63–66, 68–74, 100, 107, 110–111, 113–118, 122–123, 125, 129–131, 134–137, 141. See also denuclearization

O

Obama, Barack, xii, xiii, xiv, xv, 5, 45, 62, 78, 85–86, 88–90, 110–111, 124
oil prospecting, 40
Olympic Games, 66–67, 96–97, 113, 136
opposition, loyal, 9
orphans, 36–37
outcomes, negative, 15, 141
outcomes, positive, xvi, 14, 82
out-migration, 31–33, 129

P

Pacific Ocean, 91
Paek Nam Sun, 75
Pakistan, 69, 74, 78, 115, 134, 140
Paris Agreement on Ending the War and Restoring Peace in Vietnam (Paris Accord) (1973), 5, 8, 22–25, 38, 41, 50, 123
Paris Agreement on Cambodia (1991), 30, 41, 43, 124
Paris Conference on Cambodia, 1989, 29, 41, 53, 124
Paris Conference on Cambodia, 1991, 6, 30, 43, 124
Park Geun Hye, 67
Pashtuns, 140
payoffs, 12–13, 123–124, 128–129
peace, xi, xxi, 3, 6, 30, 50, 52, 68, 88, 123–124, 127, 134, 136, 141–142
peace agreements, 5, 8, 11, 21–25, 30, 38, 41, 43, 50, 60, 79, 98, 109, 123–124, 129
peace conferences, 1, 6, 21, 29–32, 41–43, 53, 60, 124
Peace of Westphalia (1648), 1
"peace through strength," 97
Peaceful Coexistence of Participating States pledge (2004), 79, 115
peacekeepers. See United Nations, peacekeepers
Pence, Michael, 98, 118
People's Republic of China. See China
People's Republic of Kampuchea. See Kampuchea
perquisite salaries, 39
Perry, William, xv, 73–74
Phạm Văn Đồng, 38
Philippines, 4, 24, 32, 62
plebiscite, 5, 22, 46
plutonium, 70, 72, 82, 85–86
Pol Pot, 6, 27, 28
Poland, 22, 61
political prisoners, 30, 33–34, 52–53
political unification, 5, 8, 23, 46, 52, 59, 61, 65, 67, 89, 134
Pompeo, Michael, xvii, 97–98
poverty, 32
Powell, Colin, 76
power, economic, 8, 12
power, military, xix, 1, 6, 12, 20–21, 29, 46, 59, 70, 78, 99, 121, 123, 129, 135
power, political, xi, 1, 4, 7–8, 12–13, 28–30, 34, 43, 123
power configuration, 12, 123, 131
power equality, 121–122
power sharing, 41
power vacuum, 135
predictions, 12–15, 33–34, 121–130
prejudice, 32
pre-negotiation, 14
"printing money," 39
prisoners of war, xiii–xiv, 24, 26–27, 61–62, 107, 113
private goods. See goods, private
Proliferation Security Initiative, 78, 96, 109
proliferation, missile, 68–69, 72–77, 110, 114–118, 128–129
proliferation, nuclear, 68, 75–76
"Promised Land," 139
protocol, 14, 85
psychological healing, 37
public, mass, 13, 24
public goods. See goods, public
public input, 13, 126, 128
public moods, 13
public opinion, 125–126

public place, xiii
Putin, Vladimir, 96

R

Rambo groups, 24
rapprochement, 3, 11, 15
Rational Choice Paradigm, 11–13, 121–126
reactor, light-water, 69–71, 73–74, 76–78, 80–82, 99, 108, 110, 114–115, 128–129
reactor, nuclear, 69–71, 77–78, 81–83, 116–117
reactor, plutonium, 70, 72
Reagan, Ronald, 6, 25–26, 29, 33, 35, 37, 50–51, 68, 124
reciprocation, xi, 3, 14, 99–100, 130–131, 136
recognition, diplomatic, 1, 3–9, 11–12, 19, 65, 131
rectitude, 129
refugee camps, 31
refugees, 7, 23, 28, 30, 32
refugees, economic, 7, 30, 32
refugees, political, 23, 28, 30, 32
remittances, 39–40, 51, 63, 126
reparations, 25
repatriation, 32, 129
Republic of China. See Taiwan
Republic of Korea. See South Korea
Republic of Vietnam. See South Vietnam
respect, 80, 82, 127, 129, 131
revolution, 5, 6, 7
Rhee, Syngman, 61, 67
Ri Yong Ho, xv, 96
Rice, Condoleeza, 80
Richardson, Bill, xi–xvii, xxi, 71–73, 88, 100, 127
Richardson Center for Global Engagement, xiii, xiv
Ridge, Thomas, 33
right of self-defense, 29, 94, 135
right to peaceful uses of nuclear power, 78–82, 94, 135
rivalries, international, 1, 11, 15, 121

Rodman, Dennis, 91, 96, 100, 117–118
Roh Moo Hyun, 67
Roosevelt, Franklin Delano, 7
Russia, civil war, 7
Russia, cyberwar, 9
Russia, imperial, 4
Russia, military, 133
Russia, military interventions, 7, 133
Russia, relations with Germany, 133
Russia, relations with Japan, 93
Russia, relations with North Korea, 65, 78–79, 83–86, 91–95, 97, 122, 136, 141
Russia, relations with South Korea, 93
Russia, relations with the United States, 4, 7, 9, 79, 85, 91–92, 95, 123
Russia, Vladivostok, 93
Russia. See also Soviet Union

S

saber rattling, 9, 63
"safe conduct pass," 65
Sahrawi, 1
sanctions, economic, xiii, xv, 6–8, 22–23, 32, 34, 36, 38–40, 42–43, 50, 52, 62–63, 65, 69, 73–77, 79–82, 84–96, 98, 107–112, 125, 135–136
sanctions, secondary, 89, 92
sanctions, personal, 90, 111
satellite surveillance, 65
satellites, 63, 73, 75, 85–87, 90, 110, 114, 116–117, 128
Scud-B missiles, 68
Sea of Japan, 78, 91, 115
"Second Korean War" military exercises, 64
security community, 14
Selectorate Paradigm, 12–13, 15, 123–126, 129
Serbia, 133
sewing machines, 137
Sigur, Gaston, 26
Singapore, 32, 37, 39, 92
Singapore Declaration, xxi, 62, 68, 98–100, 118, 136–137

INDEX

Singapore summit, 124, 131, 136
Six-Party Talks, xii, 78–88, 96, 108, 110, 115–117, 131, 135
skill, 129
smuggling, 39, 70, 125
socialism, 39, 124, 125
socialist countries, 38
Socialist Republic of Vietnam. See Vietnam
soldiers, dead, xvi, 19, 23–24, 26, 37, 62, 64
soldiers, disabled, 24
soldiers, experiences of, 24, 33, 40, 51, 62
soldiers, missing in action (MIAs), xiii, 23–27, 31, 34, 37, 41, 43–44, 50–53, 62, 98, 113, 126, 129
soldiers, prisoners of war (POWs), xiii, 24, 26–27, 53, 61–62, 95, 107, 113, 118
soldiers, wounded, 24, 64, 84
Solomon, Richard, xx, 41–42
Somalia, pirates, 83, 109
Somaliland, 1
South Africa, 62, 141
South China Sea, 9, 45, 122
South Korea, 56
South Korea, aerial encounter with North Korea, 66, 88, 113, 117
South Korea, anti-missile system, 88–89, 98
South Korea, Busan, 60
South Korea, constitutions, 66–67
South Korea, democratic protest (1987), 66
South Korea, economy, 63
South Korea, military, xvi, 62, 64, 68–69, 71–72, 88–89, 93, 95–100, 107–108, 110–113, 118, 128, 137
South Korea, missiles, 93, 108, 112
South Korea, national defense system (NDS), 69
South Korea, naval encounters with North Korea, 66, 73, 86–88, 94, 116
South Korea, American nuclear weapons in, 64, 68, 89, 107
South Korea, Olympic Games, 66, 96–97, 113, 136
South Korea, police, 64

South Korea, presidents, xx, 61, 66–67, 74–75, 85, 96
South Korea, refusal to accept armistice, 60–61, 67, 136
South Korea, relations with China, 5, 60, 66, 86, 88, 90
South Korea, relations with Japan, 72, 88, 93, 95
South Korea, relations with North Korea, xiv, 59–69, 72–74, 78–79, 83–84, 86–89, 91–92, 94, 96–98, 100, 113, 116, 118, 122, 136–137, 141
South Korea, relations with Poland, 61
South Korea, relations with Russia, 93
South Korea, relations with the United Nations, 59–60, 64, 66–68, 93, 96
South Korea, relations with the United States, xv, xvi, 60, 62, 64–69, 71, 87–89, 93, 95, 96–97, 100, 107, 108, 112, 116, 122, 131, 136–137, 140–141
South Korea, relations with Vietnam, 24, 40
South Korea, reunification goal, 61, 65, 89, 134
South Korea, Seoul, 57, 97, 141
South Korea, "Sunshine Policy," xx, 67
South Korea, tourists to North Korea, 67
South Korea–United States mutual defense agreement, 60, 67, 93, 107
South Korea, Yeonpeong, 66
South Korean relatives living in North Korea, 62, 67
South Ossetia, 1
South Vietnam, civil war, 5, 8, 22, 24, 36
South Vietnam, division from North, 5, 21
South Vietnam, guerrilla war, 22
South Vietnam, nongovernmental organizations, 36
South Vietnam, prime minister, 39
South Vietnam, Provisional Revolutionary Government, 22–23
South Vietnam, refusal to hold elections, 22
South Vietnam, refusal to sign Geneva Accord, 22

South Vietnam, relations with North Vietnam, 22–23
South Vietnam, relations with Cambodia, 6, 22–23, 28
South Vietnam, relations with France, 22
South Vietnam, relations with the United States, 5, 19, 22–23, 30, 38–40
South Vietnam, Republic of Vietnam, 5, 22, 33
South Vietnam, Rex Hotel, 33
South Vietnam, Saigon, 23, 27, 35, 40, 44, 46
South Vietnam, soldiers, 24, 33
South Vietnam, State of Vietnam, 22
South Vietnam, Viet Cong, 22
South Vietnam, Viet Minh presence, 22
sovereignty, 1, 29, 109, 122
Soviet Union, collapse of, 66, 68
Soviet Union, debt nonpayment, 4
Soviet Union, intelligence agents, 27
Soviet Union, military, 29, 62
Soviet Union, newspaper, 27
Soviet Union, perestroika era, 65
Soviet Union, relations with China, 28
Soviet Union, relations with North Korea, 59, 60–62, 65, 66, 68, 122
Soviet Union, relations with Vietnam, 21, 25, 27–29, 35, 37, 38, 40, 46, 122
Soviet Union, relations with the United States, 4, 19, 28, 59
Soviet Union, relations with Vietnam, 38
Soviet Union. See also Russia
Spratly Islands, 41, 45
Sri Lanka, 4
state subsidies, 39
strategic balance, 90
strategic goods, 38
strategic location, 67
"strategic patience," xv, 85, 91, 111
strategic policies, xx, 11–12, 66, 100, 121–123, 126, 129
subversion, 34
superpowers, xx, 29, 46, 99

Sweden, xiv, 4, 37, 61
Switzerland, 61. See also Geneva
Syria, 84

T

Taft, William Howard, 4
Taiwan (Republic of China), 1, 134
Taliban, 140
talks. See bargaining; negotiations
terrorism, xiv, 65–66, 75, 80, 82–84, 95, 108, 109–110, 112, 115–116
Thae Yong Ho, 135
Thai International Airlines, 35
Thailand, 32, 54
Thailand, balloons, 24
Thailand, economy, 39, 40
Thailand, military, 24, 62
Thailand, refugees, 31
Thailand, relations with Cambodia, 28–29
Thailand, relations with the United States, 24, 29
Thailand, relations with Vietnam, 40
The Interview, 134
third parties, 15
threats, xv, 1, 6, 12, 14, 35, 40, 66–67, 69–70, 73, 76–77, 80, 87–90, 92–94, 97–99, 107–109, 112–118, 121–123, 137
Tillerson, Rex, 91–94, 96
tourism, xiii, 23, 25, 34–36, 41, 50–51, 61–62, 67, 72–73, 76, 113, 126, 129
trade, xvi, 23, 34–35, 38–40, 45, 51, 63, 73, 74, 78, 80, 93, 129
trade, barter, 38
trade agreements, 8, 45, 52–53, 67
trade war threat, 89, 93, 112
tradeoffs, 122. See also exchange, quid pro quo
Transnistria, 1
travel, international. See tourism
treaties, in force, 5, 8, 22–23, 25, 30, 60, 68, 87, 93, 123, 140

treaties, proposed, 61, 64, 75, 79, 83–84, 87–89, 98, 100, 111, 115, 117–118, 122–123, 127, 136, 141
Trịnh Xuân Lăng, 41
Trump, Donald, xiii, xv–xvi, xvii, xx, 88, 67, 68, 90–99, 100, 111–112, 118, 124, 127, 129, 131, 134–136
Turkey, 62

U

Ukraine, 134
unconditional surrender, 139
unexploded bombs, 36
unification, political, 5, 8, 23, 46, 52, 59, 61, 67, 89. See also reunification
unilateral confidence-building measures, xi, 14, 46, 99–100, 130–131, 136
unilateralism, 12, 29, 77, 79–80
Union of Soviet Socialist Republics. See Soviet Union
United Kingdom. See Britain
United Nations admission, 5–6, 25, 37, 59, 65–66, 107
United Nations Children's Fund (UNICEF), 37
United Nations Command, 60–62, 64, 90
United Nations Commission for Unification and Rehabilitation of Korea (UNCURK), 59
United Nations Commission on Human Rights (UNCHR), 88
United Nations delegates, xiii, 41, 51
United Nations Development Program (UNDP), 37
United Nations General Assembly, 28, 59–60, 94, 140
United Nations headquarters, 41, 69
United Nations High Commissioner for Refugees (UNHCR), 31, 33
United Nations sanctions, 63, 69, 81, 85–89, 91–92, 94–96, 98, 108, 111–112, 115

United Nations Security Council, 28, 61, 65, 69, 81, 85, 89, 91–92, 94, 96, 108, 135
United Nations Transitional Authority for Cambodia (UNTAC), 6, 30, 42
United Nations Under Secretary-General for Political Affairs, 95
United Nations, Food and Agriculture Organization of (FAO), 37
United Nations, peacekeepers, 8, 28, 50, 60
United Nations, Uniting for Peace Resolution, 140
United Nations, World Health Organization (WHO), 37
United States, African Americans, 32
United States, Agency for International Development (USAID), 37
United States, agreement violations with North Korea, 64–66, 70, 72–74, 76–86, 88, 99, 107–111
United States, armed forces, xii, xiv–xv, 8, 22, 26, 33, 37, 45, 59, 60, 65, 66, 67, 71, 92–94, 126, 137
United States, American Defense Institute, 24
United States, American Friends Service Committee, 36
United States, American Homecoming Bill, 33, 50
United States, Arms Control Association, 68
United States, Army Central Identification Laboratory, 26
United States, "Axis of Evil" speech, 76, 109, 122
United States, back-channel talks, xvii, 5–6, 19, 50, 69, 90, 108, 109, 115
United States, banks, 38, 40
United States, Cabinet, 133
United States, California, 35, 40
United States, California State University, Fullerton, 35
United States, Case-Church Amendment, 23, 38

United States, Central Intelligence Agency (CIA), 110, 139
United States, Coalition of Families of Korean and Cold War POW/MIAs, 62
United States, Coast Guard, 45
United States, Committee for Scientific Cooperation with Vietnam, 35
United States, Congress, xx, 2, 25–26, 33, 38–39, 41, 45, 50, 71–73, 91, 112, 126, 140
United States, Cornell University, 35
United States, counterfeit currency, 81
United States, cyberhobbling, 88
United States, Department of State, 26, 41, 42, 45, 77, 88, 91–92, 119. See also United States, Secretaries of State
United States, Department of the Treasury, 8, 36–37, 40–41, 45
United States, Director of National Intelligence, 88
United States, East Coast, 118
United States, East-West Center, 35
United States, elections, xiii, 6–7, 9, 36, 65, 75–76, 79, 85, 90, 123–124, 127, 140
United States, embassies, 6, 8, 23, 27, 30, 33, 35, 44–45
United States, Export-Import Bank, 45
United States, food aid, 63, 73, 85, 87, 108, 110–111, 126, 129
United States, Foreign Service, 43
United States, Generalized System of Preferences, 45
United States, Georgetown University, 36
United States, Good Neighbor policy, 7
United States, Heritage Foundation, 34
United States, Hollywood films, 24, 88
United States, immigrant sponsors, 31
United States, independence, 139–140
United States, Institute of Peace, xix
United States, intelligence information, xiii, xiv–xv, 69, 71, 141
United States, Iran Nonproliferation Act, 76
United States, Jackson-Vanik Amendment, 39, 43, 50

United States, Joint Casualty Resolution Center, 26
United States, Joint Chiefs of Staff, 92
United States, leaflets dropped on North Korea, 65, 107
United States, economic sanctions applied, xv, 6, 22–23, 32, 34, 36, 38–40, 42–43, 45, 50, 52, 63, 65, 73–77, 80–82, 88–95, 98, 108–112, 125, 130, 135–136
United States, Hostage Recovery Fusion Cell (HRFC), xiv
United States, Lindblad Travel Agency, 36
United States, list of "rogue states," 71, 108
United States, list of state sponsors of terrorism, 65–66, 82, 84, 95, 108, 110, 112
United States, Los Angeles Times, xx
United States, Marines, 8
United States, *Mayflower*, 139
United States, media, xx, 20, 136
United States, Mennonite Central Committee, 36
United States, Monroe Doctrine, 6
United States, National League of Families of American Prisoners and Missing in Action in Southeast Asia, 26
United States, National United Front for the Liberation of Vietnam, 34
United States, negotiation concessions involving North Korea, 62–63, 65, 69–71, 73–80, 82–83, 85, 92–98, 102–111
United States, negotiation concessions involving Vietnam, 25–27, 30, 32–34, 36–37, 40–45, 50–52
United States, negotiation deviousness involving North Korea, 61–70, 72–73, 75–98, 107–113
United States, negotiation deviousness involving Vietnam, 22–29, 31, 33–34, 36–38, 40–41, 44, 50–51
United States, New York Philharmonic Orchestra, 63, 84, 110, 116, 126

INDEX

United States, New York Times, xx
United States, North Korea Sanctions and Policy Enhancement Act, 89–90
United States, nuclear weapons in South Korea, 64–65, 68–69, 89, 98, 107, 111, 113
United States, Ohio, xii, xiii, 140
United States, oil companies, 40, 46, 126
United States, Orderly Departure Program (ODP), 31, 51
United States, Oxfam America, 37
United States, Patriot missiles, 66, 108
United States, Pearl Harbor, 135
United States, policy of "strategic patience," xv, 85, 91, 111
United States, political parties, 136
United States, Postal Service, 25, 50
United States, pre-settlement orientation programs, 31
United States, Presidential Commission on Americans Missing and Unaccounted for in Southeast Asia, 25
United States, Puritan Pilgrims, 139
United States, reconnaissance airplanes (spy flights), 65
United States, "red lines," 91–93, 111
United States, relations with Cambodia, xix–xx, 6, 8, 22, 26, 28–30, 36, 41, 50–51, 122, 124, 127
United States, relations with China, 8, 19, 25, 28, 45–46, 60, 65, 78, 87, 89–93, 95, 111–112, 122, 131, 134
United States, relations with Japan, 5, 43, 52, 60, 88, 135
United States, relations with North Korea, xii, xiv–xvi, xix, 4–6, 19–20, 59–101, 107–118, 122–137
United States, relations with North Vietnam, xix–xx, 5–6, 19, 21–23, 38–39, 50, 123, 126, 131
United States, relations with Russia, 4, 7, 9, 79, 85, 91–92, 95, 123
United States, relations with South Korea, xvi–xvii, 60, 62, 64–69, 71, 87–89, 93, 95–97, 100, 107–108, 112, 116, 122, 131, 136–137, 140–141
United States, relations with South Vietnam, 5, 19, 22–23, 30, 38–40
United States, relations with Soviet Union, 4, 19, 28, 59
United States, relations with Thailand, 24, 29
United States, relations with Vietnam, xi, xvii, xix–xx, 2, 5, 8, 20, 21–46, 50–53, 121–132, 137, 140, 142
United States, resettlement services program, 23, 33, 129
United States, Richardson Center for Global Engagement, xiii–xiv
United States, schoolchildren, 37, 50
United States, Secretary of Defense, 75
United States, Secretaries of State, xvi–xvii, 28, 34, 41, 44, 73, 75–76, 80, 91–92, 94, 96, 98, 108, 110–111, 135
United States, Special Forces, 22
United States, students from Vietnam, 36
United States, Territory of Guam, 92, 96, 118
United States, trade licensing, 36–37, 41–42, 51
United States, Trading with the Enemy Act, 37, 38, 62
United States, Treasury bonds, 8
United States, UN ambassadors, xi, xv, xxi, 77–78, 95, 127, 135
United States, United States Information Agency (USIA), 36
United States, United States Indochina Reconciliation Project (USIRP), 35–36
United States, University of Hawai'i, 35–36
United States, University of Utah, 36
United States, USS *Pueblo*, 65, 113
United States, USS *Ranger*, 40–41
United States, veterans, 26, 33, 37, 126
United States, Vietnamese Americans, 35, 39–40, 44, 51, 126
United States, Voice of America, 26

United States, Washington Post, xx
United States, Westport, Connecticut, 36
United States, White House, 76, 85, 96–97
United States, world leadership, 136
United States–South Korea military exercises, xv, 64, 68–69, 71–72, 88–89, 92–93, 95–100, 107–108, 110–113, 118, 128, 137
United States–Vietnam Trade Council, 40
USA–USSR Joint Commission, 59

V

Vance, Cyrus, 28
Vessey, John A., Jr., 26, 31, 37, 51, 127, 130–131
Vienna Convention on Consular Relations, 44, 52, 53
Vietnam, 54. See also North Vietnam; South Vietnam
Vietnam, Agent Orange, 36
Vietnam, agricultural cooperatives, 39
Vietnam, Amerasians, 23, 32–33, 50
Vietnam, arms embargo, 40, 45, 52
Vietnam, balloons from Thailand, 24
Vietnam, banking, 38–40, 42, 51, 129
Vietnam, birth defects, 36
Vietnam, black market, 39
Vietnam, "boat people," 32, 53
Vietnam, bomb craters, 36
Vietnam, bribery, 31
Vietnam, bureaucracy, 31
Vietnam, Cam Ranh Bay, 44, 45, 132
Vietnam, central bank, 39
Vietnam, civil war, 5, 8, 22, 24, 52, 140
Vietnam, coast guard, 31
Vietnam, coastline, 126
Vietnam, colony of France, 5, 21, 59, 140
Vietnam, Communist Party, 39
Vietnam, Council of Ministers, 35
Vietnam, credit, 45
Vietnam, currency, 39
Vietnam, Danang, 45

Vietnam, defoliation, 36
Vietnam, demilitarized zone, 21
Vietnam, division, 21–22, 142
Vietnam, Democratic Republic of. See North Vietnam
Vietnam, Đổi Mới reforms, 38–39, 125
Vietnam, dual citizenship, 44
Vietnam, economic aid, 23–26, 36–39, 41, 43–45, 50–52
Vietnam, economic migrants, 32
Vietnam, economy, 34–40
Vietnam, embassies, 35, 44–45
Vietnam, emperor of, 22
Vietnam, equidistance policy, 28
Vietnam, ethnic Chinese, 30
Vietnam, exchange rates, 39
Vietnam, farmland, 36
Vietnam, fishing, 45
Vietnam, foreign exchange reserve, 40
Vietnam, Foreign Ministry, 27
Vietnam, forests, 36
Vietnam, frozen assets, 38, 45, 52
Vietnam, government bonds, 44
Vietnam, Hanoi, 21, 35, 37, 42, 44, 51, 53, 55
Vietnam, "healing the wounds of war," 23–27, 37
Vietnam, Ho Chi Minh City, 23, 28, 32–33, 35, 37, 40, 51, 53
Vietnam, human rights, 44–45, 51
Vietnam, humanitarian aid, 23, 34, 36–37, 44, 46
Vietnam, insurance, 45
Vietnam, International Control Commission, 22
Vietnam, international mail, 25
Vietnam, international students, 36
Vietnam, investment, 23, 38–40, 43–44
Vietnam, judiciary, 31, 44
Vietnam, land mines, 36
Vietnam, loans, 38, 42–43, 51
Vietnam, mangroves, 36
Vietnam, medical assistance, 37, 129
Vietnam, missing persons in action (MIAs), 24–26, 46

Vietnam, Ministry of Tourism, 35
Vietnam, national income, 39
Vietnam, national power, 121, 129
Vietnam, navy, 31
Vietnam, negotiation concessions with the United States, 25–27, 29, 30, 32–35, 40–44, 52–53
Vietnam, negotiation deviousness with the United States, 23–27, 31, 33, 44, 52
Vietnam, northern border, 23, 38–39
Vietnam, nuclear power, 45
Vietnam, Office for Seeking Missing Persons, 24
Vietnam, oil concessions, 38, 40, 46
Vietnam, Orderly Departure Program, 31, 33, 50–53
Vietnam, orphans, 37
Vietnam, out-migration, 31–34, 129
Vietnam, People's Army of Vietnam (PAVN), 6, 19, 21, 23–24, 26, 28–29, 38, 40–41, 46, 125, 127
Vietnam, Perfume River, 21
Vietnam, plebiscite, 5, 22, 46, 50
Vietnam, political reeducation, 33–34
Vietnam, prime ministers, 35
Vietnam, private aid, 25–26, 37, 51
Vietnam, Provisional Revolutionary Government of. See Vietnam, Viet Cong
Vietnam, racial prejudice, 32
Vietnam, reconstruction, 23–25, 38, 41
Vietnam, re-education camps, 34
Vietnam, refugees, 23, 30–32
Vietnam, relations with Cambodia, 22, 25–30, 38, 42, 46, 50, 52–53, 122, 124–125, 127, 129–130
Vietnam, relations with China, 8, 19, 28–30, 32, 46, 122
Vietnam, relations with France, 21–22, 29, 40–42, 51, 140
Vietnam, relations with Japan, 5, 21, 39–40, 43, 52, 140
Vietnam, relations with South Korea, 24, 40
Vietnam, relations with the Soviet Union, 38
Vietnam, relations with Thailand, 40

Vietnam, relations with the United Nations, 25, 28, 37, 50
Vietnam, relations with the United States, xi, xvii, xix–xx, 2, 5, 8, 20–46, 50–53, 121–132, 137, 140, 142
Vietnam, remittances, 40, 51, 126
Vietnam, Republic of. See South Vietnam
Vietnam, rice farmers, 39
Vietnam, rubber plantations, 38
Vietnam, rural residents, 27
Vietnam, scholars, 35
Vietnam, schoolchildren, 37, 50, 129
Vietnam, schools, 37
Vietnam, sewing machines, 37
Vietnam, smuggling, 39
Vietnam, soldiers. See Vietnam, People's Army of Vietnam
Vietnam, State of. See South Vietnam
Vietnam, taxes, 39
Vietnam, technical assistance, 42, 52, 129
Vietnam, tourism and travel, 23, 25, 34–36, 41, 50
Vietnam, trade, 23, 35, 38–40, 42–43, 45, 51–53
Vietnam, unification, 5, 8, 23, 46, 52
Vietnam, unexploded ordinance, 36
Vietnam, university curriculum, 40
Vietnam, University of Hanoi, 35–36
Vietnam, Viet Minh, 22
Vietnam, visas, 31–32, 35, 53
Vietnam, war casualties, 24, 26, 36, 37, 139
Vietnam, withdrawal from Cambodia, 29, 53, 127, 129
Vietnam–United States Trade Council, 40
Villa, Pancho, 7–8

W

war, devastation from, 12, 24–25, 36, 62, 94
war, independence, 4, 139
war, nuclear, 88, 113, 115
war, preventive, 92
war, proxy, 8, 28–29
war, technical, 6, 8, 60, 136

war games. *See* United States-South Korean military exercises
war legacy, 33
war. *See also* civil wars; cyberwar; guerrilla war; Korean War; trade war
Warmbier, Otto, xii, 100
wealth, 31, 125, 129
well-being, 129
wheelchairs, 37
Wilson, Woodrow, 4, 7–8
Woodcock, Leonard, 25, 28
World Bank, 38, 42–43, 52, 63
world economy. *See* economy, global
World War I, 7–8, 133–134
World War II, xix, 5, 21, 59, 133, 135
World War III, 132, 133–137
"wounds of war," 23, 24–27, 61–63

Z

Zakaria, Fareed, xx